Sign Up Online

GMAS

Grade 6 Math Practice

Get Digital Access To

2 GMAS Practice Tests

5 Math Domains

Register Now

Url: www.lumoslearning.com/a/tedbooks

Access Code: GMASG6M-18253-P

Georgia Milestones Assessment System Test Prep: 6th Grade Math Practice Workbook and Full-length Online Assessments: GMAS Study Guide

Contributing Author	-	**Renee Bade**
Contributing Author	-	**Kimberly G.**
Executive Producer	-	**Mukunda Krishnaswamy**
Designer and Illustrator	-	**Sowmya R.**

First Edition - 2020

ISBN-10: 1-945730-75-7

ISBN-13: 978-1-945730-75-7

Printed in the United States of America

Last updated - July 2022

For permissions and additional information contact us

Lumos Information Services, LLC
PO Box 1575, Piscataway, NJ 08855-1575
http://www.LumosLearning.com

Email: support@lumoslearning.com
Tel: (732) 384-0146
Fax: (866) 283-6471

Lumos Learning
Developed by Expert Teachers

INTRODUCTION

About Lumos tedBook for GMAS Test Practice:
This book is specifically designed to improve student achievement on the GMAS. Students perform at their best on standardized tests when they feel comfortable with the test content as well as the test format. Lumos tedBook for GMAS test ensures this with meticulously designed practice that adheres to the guidelines provided by the GMAS for the number of questions, standards, difficulty level, sessions, question types, and duration.

About Lumos Smart Test Prep:
With more than a decade of experience and expertise in developing practice resources for standardized tests, Lumos Learning has developed the most efficient methodology to help students succeed on the state assessments (See Figure 1).

Lumos Smart Test Prep Methodology offers students realistic GMAS assessment rehearsal along with providing an efficient pathway to overcome each proficiency gap.

The process starts with students taking the online diagnostic assessment. This online diagnostic test will help assess students' proficiency levels in various standards. With the completion of this diagnostic assessment, Lumos generates a personalized study plan with a standard checklist based on student performance in the online diagnostic test. Parents and educators can use this study plan to remediate the proficiency gaps with targeted standards-based practice available in the workbook.

After student completes the targeted remedial practice, they should attempt the second online GMAS practice test. Upon finishing the second assessment, Lumos will generate another individualized study plan by identifying topics that require more practice. Based on these practice suggestions, further skill building activities can be planned to help students gain comprehensive mastery needed to ensure success on the state assessment.

Lumos Smart Test Prep Methodology

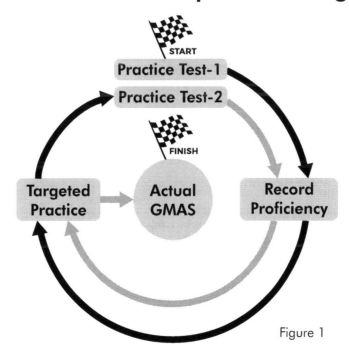

Figure 1

Table of Contents

Chapter 1

Lumos Smart Test Prep Methodology

Step 1: Access Online GMAS Practice Test

The online GMAS practice tests mirror the actual Georgia Milestones Assessment System (GMAS) in the number of questions, item types, test duration, test tools, and more.

After completing the test, your student will receive immediate feedback with detailed reports on standards mastery and a personalized study plan to overcome any learning gaps. With this study plan, use the next section of the workbook to practice.

Use the URL and access code provided below or scan the QR code to access the first GMAS practice test to get started.

URL	QR Code
Visit the URL below and place the book access code **www.lumoslearning.com/a/tedbooks** **Access Code: GMASG6M-18253-P**	

Step-2: Review the Personalized Study Plan Online

After students complete the online Practice Test 1, they can access their individualized study plan from the table of contents (Figure 2) Parents and Teachers can also review the study plan through their Lumos account (parent or teacher) portal.

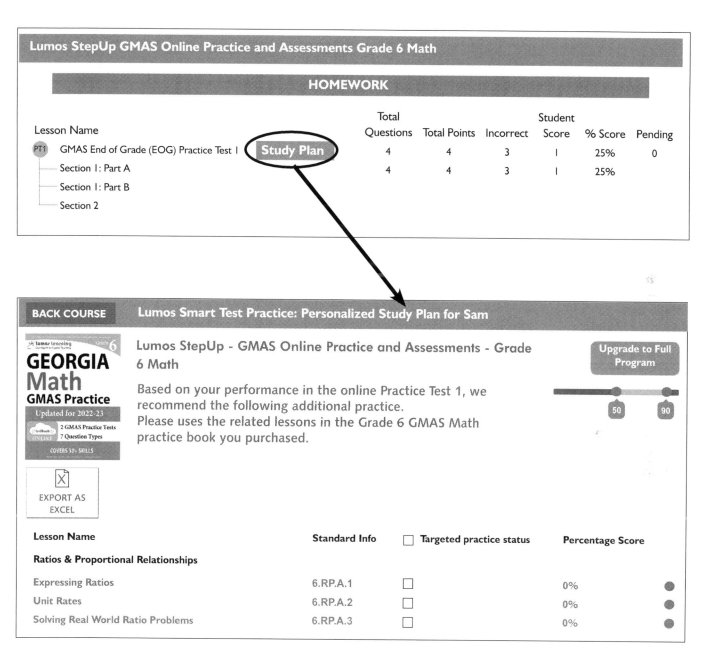

Figure 2

Step 3: Complete Targeted Practice

Using the information provided in the study plan report, complete the targeted practice using the appropriate lessons to overcome proficiency gaps. With lesson names included in the study plan, find the appropriate topics in this workbook and answer the questions provided. Students can refer to the answer key and detailed answers provided for each lesson to gain further understanding of the learning objective. Marking the completed lessons in the study plan after each practice session is recommended.(See Figure 3)

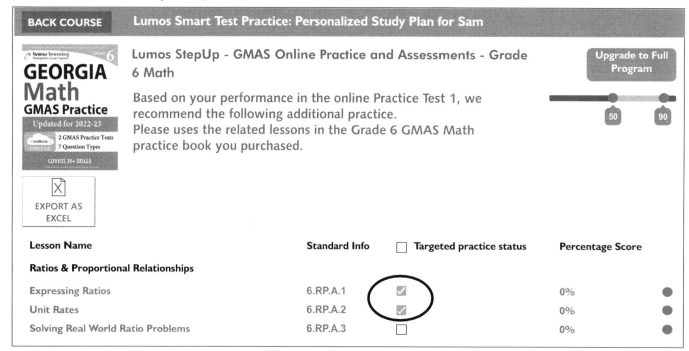

BACK COURSE	**Lumos Smart Test Practice: Personalized Study Plan for Sam**			

Lumos StepUp - GMAS Online Practice and Assessments - Grade 6 Math

Based on your performance in the online Practice Test 1, we recommend the following additional practice.
Please uses the related lessons in the Grade 6 GMAS Math practice book you purchased.

Upgrade to Full Program

50   90

EXPORT AS EXCEL

Lesson Name	Standard Info	☐ Targeted practice status	Percentage Score	
Ratios & Proportional Relationships				
Expressing Ratios	6.RP.A.1	☑	0%	●
Unit Rates	6.RP.A.2	☑	0%	●
Solving Real World Ratio Problems	6.RP.A.3	☐	0%	●

Figure 3

Step 4: Access the Practice Test 2 Online

After completing the targeted practice in this workbook, students should attempt the second GMAS practice test online. Using the student login name and password, login to the Lumos website to complete the second practice test.

Step 5: Repeat Targeted Practice

Repeat the targeted practice as per Step 3 using the second study plan report for Practice test 2 after completion of the second GMAS rehearsal.

Visit www.lumoslearning.com/a/lstp for more information on Lumos Smart Test Prep Methodology or Scan the QR Code

What if I buy more than one Lumos Study Program?

Step 1 ⟶ **Visit the URL given below and login to your account**

www.lumoslearning.com

Step 2 ⟶ **Click on 'My tedBooks' under the "Account" tab**

Place the Book Access Code and submit.

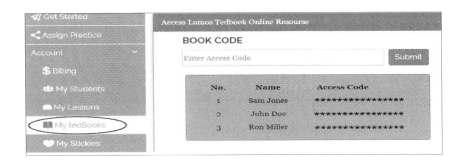

Step 3 ⟶ **Add the new book**

To add the new book for a registered student, choose the '**Existing Student**' button, select the student and submit.

To add the new book for a new student, choose the '**Add New Student**' button and complete the student registration.

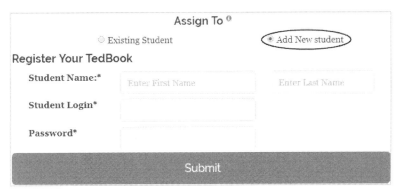

Test Taking Tips

1) **The day before the test,** make sure you get a good night's sleep.

2) **On the day of the test,** be sure to eat a good hearty breakfast! Also, be sure to arrive at school on time.

3) **During the test:**

- **Read each question carefully.**

    - Do not spend too much time on any one question. Work steadily through all questions in the section.
    - Attempt all the questions even if you are not sure of some answers.
    - If you run into a difficult question, eliminate as many choices as you can and then pick the best one from the remaining choices. Intelligent guessing will help you increase your score.
    - Also, mark the question so that if you have extra time, you can return to it after you reach the end of the section.
    - Some questions may refer to a graph, chart, or other kind of picture. Carefully review the infographics before answering the question.
    - Be sure to include explanations for your written responses and show all work.

- **While Answering Multiple-choice (EBSR) questions.**

    - Select the bubble corresponding to your answer choice.
    - Read all of the answer choices, even if think you have found the correct answer.

- **While Answering TECR questions.**

    - Read the directions of each question. Some might ask you to drag something, others to select, and still others to highlight. Follow all instructions of the question (or questions if it is in multiple parts)

Chapter 2:
Ratios & Proportional Relationships

Lesson 1: Expressing Ratios

You can scan the QR code given below or use the url to access additional EdSearch resources including videos and mobile apps related to *Expressing Ratios*.

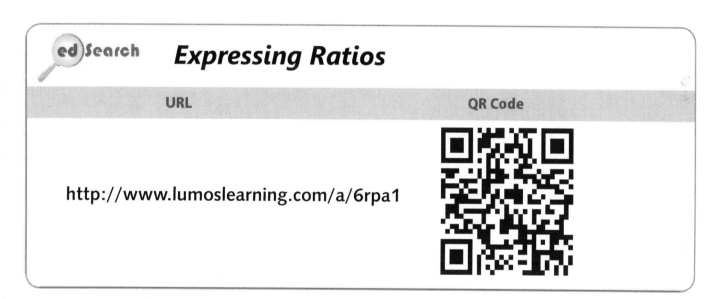

ed)Search **Expressing Ratios**	
URL	QR Code
http://www.lumoslearning.com/a/6rpa1	

1. **A school has an enrollment of 600 students. 330 of the students are girls. Express the fraction of students who are boys in simplest terms.**

   Ⓐ $\dfrac{12}{20}$

   Ⓑ $\dfrac{11}{20}$

   Ⓒ $\dfrac{9}{20}$

   Ⓓ $\dfrac{13}{20}$

2. **In the 14th century, the Sultan of Brunei noticed that his ratio of emeralds to rubies was the same as the ratio of diamonds to pearls. If he had 85 emeralds, 119 rubies, and 45 diamonds, how many pearls did he have?**

   Ⓐ 17
   Ⓑ 22
   Ⓒ 58
   Ⓓ 63

3. **Mr. Fullingham has 75 geese and 125 turkeys. What is the ratio of the number of geese to the total number of birds in simplest terms?**

   Ⓐ 75:200
   Ⓑ 3:8
   Ⓒ 125:200
   Ⓓ 5:8

4. **The little league team called the Hawks has 7 brunettes, 5 blonds, and 2 redheads. What is the ratio of redheads to the entire team in simplest terms?**

   Ⓐ 2:7
   Ⓑ 2:5
   Ⓒ 2:12
   Ⓓ 1:7

5. The little league team called the Hawks has 7 brunettes, 5 blonds, and 2 redheads. The entire little league division that the Hawks belong to has the same ratio of redheads to everyone else. What is the total number of redheads in that division if the total number of players is 126?

    Ⓐ 9
    Ⓑ 14
    Ⓒ 18
    Ⓓ 24

6. Barnaby decided to count the number of ducks and geese flying south for the winter. The first day he counted 175 ducks and 63 geese. What is the ratio of ducks to the total number of birds flying overhead in simplest terms?

    Ⓐ 175:63
    Ⓑ 175:238
    Ⓒ 25:9
    Ⓓ 25:34

7. Barnaby decided to count the number of ducks and geese flying south for the winter. The first day he counted 175 ducks and 63 geese. By the end of migration, Barnaby had counted 4,725 geese. If the ratio of ducks to geese remained the same (175 to 63), how many ducks did he count?

    Ⓐ 13,125
    Ⓑ 17,850
    Ⓒ 10,695
    Ⓓ 14,750

8. Barbara was baking a cake and could not find her tablespoon measure. The recipe calls for $3\frac{1}{3}$ tablespoons. Each table spoon measure 3 teaspoon. How many teaspoons must Barbara use in order to have the recipe turn out all right?

    Ⓐ 3
    Ⓑ 6
    Ⓒ 9
    Ⓓ 10

9. The ratio of girls to boys in a grade is 6 to 5. If there are 24 girls in the grade then how many students are there altogether?

    Ⓐ 14
    Ⓑ 24
    Ⓒ 34
    Ⓓ 44

10. The ratio of pencils to pens in a box is 3 to 2. If there are 30 pencils and pens altogether, how many pencils are there?

   Ⓐ 16
   Ⓑ 17
   Ⓒ 18
   Ⓓ 19

11. Which of the following correctly expresses the ratio of shaded bows to the number of total bows? Select all answers that apply.

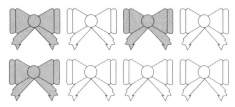

   Ⓐ 3:8
   Ⓑ 5:8
   Ⓒ $\dfrac{3}{5}$
   Ⓓ $\dfrac{3}{8}$
   Ⓔ $\dfrac{5}{8}$

12. Write the ratio that correctly describes the number of white stars compared to the number of gray stars. Write your answer in the box below.

13. Complete the following table by filling in the blanks with a number that shows the correct ratio that is equivalent to the one shown in the first row.

1	2
2	4
	6
4	8
5	
	12

Chapter 2

Lesson 2: Unit Rates

You can scan the QR code given below or use the url to access additional EdSearch resources including videos and mobile apps related to *Unit Rates*.

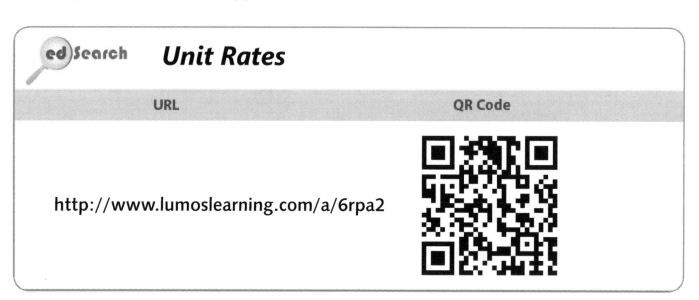

ed Search   *Unit Rates*

URL	QR Code
http://www.lumoslearning.com/a/6rpa2	

1. **Which is a better price: 5 for $1.00, 4 for 85¢, 2 for 25¢, or 6 for $1.10?**

    Ⓐ 5 for $1.00
    Ⓑ 4 for 85¢
    Ⓒ 2 for 25¢
    Ⓓ 6 for $1.10

2. **At grocery Store A, 5 cans of baked beans cost $3.45. At grocery Store B, 7 cans of baked beans cost $5.15. At grocery Store C, 4 cans of baked beans cost $2.46. At grocery Store D, 6 cans of baked beans cost $4.00. How much money would you save if you bought 20 cans of baked beans from grocery store C than if you bought 20 cans of baked beans from grocery store A?**

    Ⓐ $1.75
    Ⓑ $1.25
    Ⓒ $1.50
    Ⓓ 95¢

3. **Beverly drove from Atlantic City to Newark. She drove for 284 miles at a constant speed of 58 mph. How long did it take Beverly to complete the trip?**

    Ⓐ 4 hours and 45 minutes
    Ⓑ 4 hours and 54 minutes
    Ⓒ 4 hours and 8 minutes
    Ⓓ 4 hours and 89 minutes

4. **Don has two jobs. For Job 1, he earns $7.55 an hour. For Job 2, he earns $8.45 an hour. Last week he worked at the first job for 10 hours and at the second job for 15 hours. What were his average earnings per hour?**

    Ⓐ $8.00
    Ⓑ $8.09
    Ⓒ $8.15
    Ⓓ $8.13

5. **It took Marjorie 15 minutes to drive from her house to her daughter's school. If the school was 4 miles away from her house, what was her unit rate of speed?**

    Ⓐ 16 mph
    Ⓑ 8 mph
    Ⓒ 4 mph
    Ⓓ 30 mph

6. The Belmont race track known as "Big Sandy" is 1½ miles long. In 1973, Secretariat won the Belmont Stakes race in 2 minutes and 30 seconds. Assuming he ran on "Big Sandy", what was his unit speed?

   Ⓐ 30 mph
   Ⓑ 40 mph
   Ⓒ 36 mph
   Ⓓ 38 mph

7. If 1 pound of chocolate creams at Philadelphia Candies costs $7.52. How much does that candy cost by the ounce?

   Ⓐ 48¢ per oz.
   Ⓑ 47¢ per oz.
   Ⓒ 75.2¢ per oz.
   Ⓓ 66¢ per oz.

8. If Carol pays $62.90 to fill the 17-gallon gas tank in her vehicle and she can drive 330 miles on one tank of gas, about how much does she pay per mile to drive her vehicle?

   Ⓐ $0.37
   Ⓑ $3.70
   Ⓒ $0.19
   Ⓓ $0.01

9. A 13 ounce box of cereal costs $3.99. What is the unit price per pound?

   Ⓐ about $1.23
   Ⓑ about $2.66
   Ⓒ about $4.30
   Ⓓ about $4.91

10. A bottle of perfume costs $26.00 for a $\frac{1}{2}$ ounce bottle. What is the price per ounce?

    Ⓐ $25.50
    Ⓑ $26.50
    Ⓒ $52.00
    Ⓓ $13.00

11. Check the box in each row that represents the correct unit rate for each situation.

	1:10	1:5	1:50	1:20
$1.00 per 5 pounds	○	○	○	○
50 pounds per box	○	○	○	○
10 miles per gallon	○	○	○	○
1 lap in 20 minutes	○	○	○	○

12. Below is a recipe for Grandma Grittle's favorite cupcakes. Which of the following correctly expresses a ratio found in the recipe? Check all answers that apply.

Ingredients for 12 cupcakes:
White flour - 2 cups
Sugar - 1 cup
Baking powder - 2 tsp.
Salt - 1 tsp.
Butter or margarine - 1/3 cup
Milk - 2/3 cup
Vanilla - 1 tsp.
Semi-sweet chocolate - 1 bar

Ⓐ sugar and flour, 1:2
Ⓑ flour and total cupcakes, 1:12
Ⓒ vanilla and salt, 1:1
Ⓓ salt and baking powder, 1:2
Ⓔ chocolate to total cupcakes, 1:24

13. The bag of apples shown in the picture, costs $3.20. The cost of one apple is _____.

Chapter 2

Lesson 3: Solving Real World Ratio Problems

You can scan the QR code given below or use the url to access additional EdSearch resources including videos and mobile apps related to Solving *Real World Ratio Problems*.

edSearch

Solving Real World Ratio Problems

URL	QR Code
http://www.lumoslearning.com/a/6rpa3	

1. **How many kilograms are there in 375 grams?**

   Ⓐ 3,750 kg
   Ⓑ 37.5 kg
   Ⓒ 3.75 kg
   Ⓓ 0.375 kg

2. **How many inches are there in 2 yards?**

   Ⓐ 24 in
   Ⓑ 36 in
   Ⓒ 48 in
   Ⓓ 72 in

3. **What is 50% of 120?**

   Ⓐ 50
   Ⓑ 60
   Ⓒ 70
   Ⓓ 55

4. **Michael Jordan is six feet 6 inches tall. How much is that in inches?**

   Ⓐ 66 inches
   Ⓑ 76 inches
   Ⓒ 86 inches
   Ⓓ 78 inches

5. **What is 7.5% in decimal notation?**

   Ⓐ 0.75
   Ⓑ 0.075
   Ⓒ 0.0075
   Ⓓ 7.5

6. **A $60 shirt is on sale for 30% off. How much is the shirt's sale price?**

   Ⓐ $30
   Ⓑ $40
   Ⓒ $18
   Ⓓ $42

7. On Monday, 6 out of every 10 people who entered a store purchased something. If 1,000 people entered the store on Monday, how many people purchased something?

   Ⓐ 6 people
   Ⓑ 60 people
   Ⓒ 600 people
   Ⓓ 610 people

8. If a pair of pants that normally sells for $51.00 is now on sale for $34.00, by what percentage was the price reduced?

   Ⓐ 30%
   Ⓑ 60%
   Ⓒ 33.33%
   Ⓓ 66.67%

9. If Comic Book World is taking 28% off the comic books that normally sell for $4.00, how much money is Kevin saving if he buys 12 comic books during the sale?

   Ⓐ $28
   Ⓑ $12
   Ⓒ $13.44
   Ⓓ $14.58

10. Eric spends 45 minutes getting to work and 45 minutes returning home. What percent of the day does Eric spend commuting?

   Ⓐ 6.25%
   Ⓑ 7.8%
   Ⓒ 5.95%
   Ⓓ 15%

11. 75% of the crowd at a sports rally were wearing the team colors. If 222 people were wearing the team colors, how many people were in the crowd? Circle the correct answer choice.

   Ⓐ 74
   Ⓑ 300
   Ⓒ 296
   Ⓓ 314

12. To make yummy fruit punch, use 2 cups of grape juice for every 3 cups of apple juice. Select all of the juice combinations below that correctly follow this recipe ratio.

Ⓐ 4 cups grape juice: 6 cups apple juice
Ⓑ 5 cups grape juice: 10 cups apple juice
Ⓒ 6 cups grape juice: 9 cups apple juice
Ⓓ 6 cups grape juice: 12 cups apple juice
Ⓔ All of the above

13. Look at the ratio information found in the table below. Complete the table by correctly filling in the missing information.

Feet	Yards
3	1
6	
	3
15	5
24	

Chapter 2

Lesson 4: Solving Unit Rate Problems

You can scan the QR code given below or use the url to access additional EdSearch resources including videos and mobile apps related to *Solving Unit Rate Problems*.

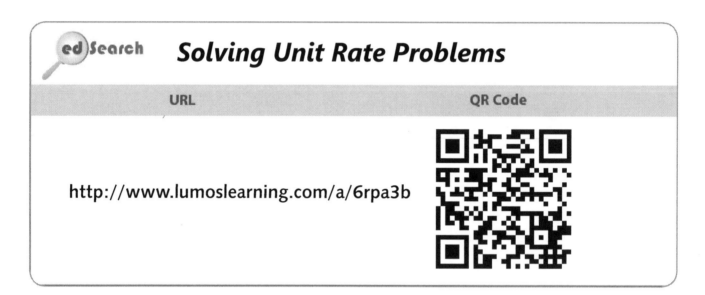

ed Search   **Solving Unit Rate Problems**

URL	QR Code
http://www.lumoslearning.com/a/6rpa3b	

1. A 12 pack of juice pouches costs $6.00. How much does one juice pouch cost?

   Ⓐ $0.02
   Ⓑ $0.20
   Ⓒ $0.50
   Ⓓ $0.72

2. Eli can ride his scooter 128 miles on one tank of gas. If the scooter has a 4-gallon gas tank, how far can Eli ride on one gallon of gas?

   Ⓐ 64 miles per gallon
   Ⓑ 32 miles per gallon
   Ⓒ 512 miles per gallon
   Ⓓ 20 miles per gallon

3. Clifton ran 6 miles in 39 minutes. At this rate, how much time Clifton takes to run one mile?

   Ⓐ 13 minutes
   Ⓑ 12 minutes
   Ⓒ 7.2 minutes
   Ⓓ 6 minutes and 30 seconds

4. Brad has swimming practice 3 days a week. This week Brad swam a total of 114 laps. At this rate how many laps did Brad swim each day?

   Ⓐ 38 laps
   Ⓑ 42 laps
   Ⓒ 57 laps
   Ⓓ 61 laps

5. Karen bought a total of seven items at five different stores. She began with $65.00 and had $15.00 remaining. Which of the following equation can be used to determine the average cost per item?

   Ⓐ $7x \times 5 = \$50.00$
   Ⓑ $7x = \$75.00$
   Ⓒ $7x + \$15.00 = \$65.00$
   Ⓓ $5x = \$65.00 - \$15.00$

6. Geoff goes to the archery range five days a week. He must pay $1.00 for every ten arrows that he shoots. If he spent $15.00 this week on arrows what is the average number of arrows Geoff shot per day?

   Ⓐ 3 arrows
   Ⓑ 30 arrows
   Ⓒ 45 arrows
   Ⓓ 75 arrows

7. Julia made 7 batches of cookies and ate 3 cookies. There were 74 cookies left. Which expression can be used to determine the average number of cookies per batch?

   Ⓐ 74÷7
   Ⓑ (74+7)÷3
   Ⓒ $\dfrac{74 + 3}{7}$
   Ⓓ $\dfrac{74}{3} \times 7$

8. Lars delivered 124 papers in 3 hours. How long did it take Lars to deliver one paper?

   Ⓐ 1 minute
   Ⓑ 1 minute and 27 seconds
   Ⓒ 1 minute and 45 seconds
   Ⓓ 2 minutes and 3 seconds

9. Mr. and Mrs. Fink met their son Conrad at the beach. Mr. and Mrs. Fink drove 462 miles on 21 gallons of fuel. Conrad drove 456 miles on 12 gallons of fuel. How many more miles per gallon does Conrad's car get than Mr. and Mrs. Fink's car?

   Ⓐ 6 mpg
   Ⓑ 22 mpg
   Ⓒ 16 mpg
   Ⓓ 38 mpg

10. Myka bought a box of 30 greeting cards for $4.00. Chuck bought a box of 100 greeting cards for $12.00. Who got the better deal?

   Ⓐ Myka got the better deal at about 13 cents per card.
   Ⓑ Myka got the better deal at about 7.5 cents per card.
   Ⓒ Chuck got the better deal at about 8 cents per card.
   Ⓓ Chuck got the better deal at 12 cents per card.

11. John paid $15 for 3 cheeseburgers. What is the rate of one cheeseburger? Enter your answer in the box below.

$

12. Tommy charges the same rate for each yard he mows. Calculate the rate he charges, then complete the missing information in the table.

Day	Total Money Earned $	Yards Mowed
Monday	50	2
Wednesday		3
Friday	25	
Saturday		5

13. A movie theatre charges $10 for a ticket. Check the box in each row that represents how much money the theatre would make from ticket sales.

	$150	$10	$100	$200
10	☐	☐	☐	☐
15	☐	☐	☐	☐
20	☐	☐	☐	☐
1	☐	☐	☐	☐

Chapter 2

Lesson 5: Finding Percent

You can scan the QR code given below or use the url to access additional EdSearch resources including videos and mobile apps related to *Finding Percent*.

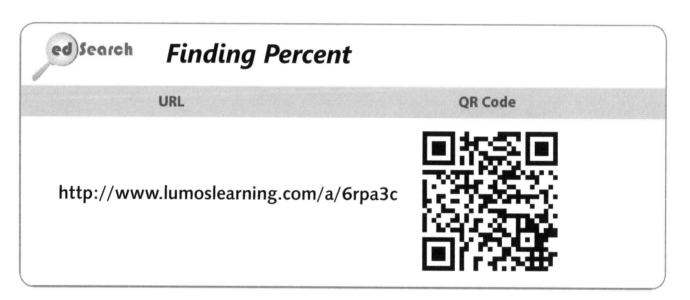

ed Search	**Finding Percent**	
URL		**QR Code**
http://www.lumoslearning.com/a/6rpa3c		

1. **What is 25% of 24?**

   Ⓐ 5
   Ⓑ 6
   Ⓒ 11
   Ⓓ 17

2. **What is 15% of 60?**

   Ⓐ 9
   Ⓑ 12
   Ⓒ 15
   Ⓓ 25

3. **9 is what percent of 72?**

   Ⓐ 7.2%
   Ⓑ 8%
   Ⓒ 12.5%
   Ⓓ 14%

4. **How much is 30% of 190?**

   Ⓐ 45
   Ⓑ 57
   Ⓒ 60
   Ⓓ 63

5. **Daniel has 280 baseball cards. 15% of these are highly collectable. How many baseball cards does Daniel possess that are highly collectable?**

   Ⓐ 15 cards
   Ⓑ 19 cards
   Ⓒ 42 cards
   Ⓓ 47 cards

6. **The football team consumed 80% of the water provided at the game. If the team consumed 8-gallons of water, how much water was provided?**

   Ⓐ 10 gallons
   Ⓑ 12 gallons
   Ⓒ 15 gallons
   Ⓓ 18.75 gallons

7. Joshua brought 156 of his 678 Legos to Emily's house. What percentage of his Legos did Joshua bring?

    Ⓐ 4%

    Ⓑ 23%

    Ⓒ 30%

    Ⓓ 43%

8. At batting practice Alexis hit 8 balls out of 15 into the outfield. Which equation below can be used to determine the percentage of balls hit into the outfield?

    Ⓐ $\dfrac{15}{8} = \dfrac{x}{100}$

    Ⓑ $\dfrac{15}{100} = \dfrac{x}{8}$

    Ⓒ $8x = (100)(15)$

    Ⓓ $\dfrac{15}{8} = \dfrac{100}{x}$

9. Nikki grows roses, tulips, and carnations. She has 78 flowers of which 32% are roses. Approximately how many roses does Nikki have?

    Ⓐ 18 roses

    Ⓑ 25 roses

    Ⓒ 28 roses

    Ⓓ 41 roses

10. Victor took out 30% of his construction paper. Of this, Paul used 6 sheets, Allison used 8 sheets and Victor and Gayle used the last ten sheets. How many sheets of construction paper did Victor not take out?

    Ⓐ 24 sheets

    Ⓑ 50 sheets

    Ⓒ 56 sheets

    Ⓓ 80 sheets

11. The following items were bought on sale. Complete the missing information.

Item Purchased	Original Price	Amount of Discount	Amount Paid
Video Game	$80	20%	
Movie Ticket	$14		$11.20
Laptop	$1,000		$750
Shoes	$55.00	10%	$49.5

12. Which of these represent 25 percent of the beginning number? Select all that apply.

Ⓐ $90, $22.50
Ⓑ $150, $15.00
Ⓒ $400, $300.00
Ⓓ $560.00, $140.00

Chapter 2

Lesson 6: Measurement Conversion

You can scan the QR code given below or use the url to access additional EdSearch resources including videos and mobile apps related to *Measurement Conversion*.

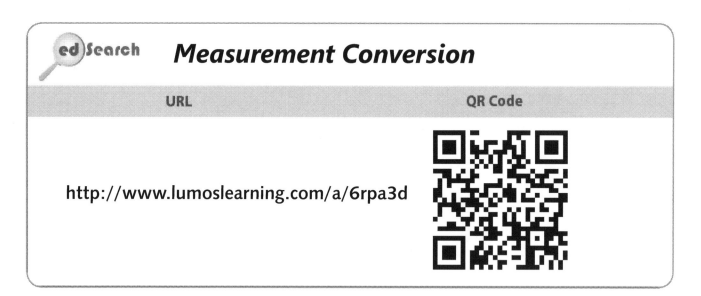

ed Search **Measurement Conversion**

URL	QR Code
http://www.lumoslearning.com/a/6rpa3d	

1. **Owen is 69 inches tall. How tall is Owen in feet?**

   Ⓐ 5.2 feet
   Ⓑ 5.75 feet
   Ⓒ 5.9 feet
   Ⓓ 6 feet

2. **What is 7 gallons 3 quarts expressed as quarts?**

   Ⓐ 4.75 quarts
   Ⓑ 28 quarts
   Ⓒ 29.2 quarts
   Ⓓ 31 quarts

3. **How many centimeters in 3.7 kilometers?**

   Ⓐ 0.000037 cm
   Ⓑ 0.037 cm
   Ⓒ 3700 cm
   Ⓓ 370,000 cm

4. **136 ounces is how many pounds?**

   Ⓐ 6.8 pounds
   Ⓑ 8.5 pounds
   Ⓒ 1088 pounds
   Ⓓ 2,176 pounds

5. **How many ounces in 5 gallons?**

   Ⓐ 128 ounces
   Ⓑ 320 ounces
   Ⓒ 640 ounces
   Ⓓ 1280 ounces

6. **Lisa, Susan, and Chris participated in a three-person relay team. Lisa ran 1284 meters, Susan ran 1635 meters and Chris ran 1473 meters. How long was the race in kilometers? Round your answer to the nearest tenth.**

   Ⓐ 4.0 km
   Ⓑ 4.4 km
   Ⓒ 43.9 km
   Ⓓ 49.0 km

7. **Quita recorded the amount of time it took her to complete her chores each week for a month; 1 hour 3 minutes, 1 hour 18 minutes, 55 minutes, and 68 minutes. How many hours did Quita spend doing chores during the month?**

    (A) 3.8 hours
    (B) 4.24 hours
    (C) 4.4 hours
    (D) 5.7 hours

8. **Lamar can run 3 miles in 18 minutes. At this rate, how much distance he can run in one hour?**

    (A) 0.9 mph
    (B) 1.1 mph
    (C) 10 mph
    (D) 21 mph

9. **A rectangular garden has a width of 67 inches and a length of 92 inches. What is the perimeter of the garden in feet?**

    (A) 13.25 feet
    (B) 26.5 feet
    (C) 31.8 feet
    (D) 42.8 feet

10. **Pat has a pen pal in England. When Pat asked how tall his pen pal was he replied, 1.27 meters. If 1 inch is 2.54 cm, how tall is Pat's pen pal in feet and inches?**

    (A) 3 feet 11 inches
    (B) 4 feet 2 inches
    (C) 4 feet 6 inches
    (D) 5 feet exactly

11. **How many fluid ounces are there in a cup? Circle the correct answer choice.**

    (A) 10 fl oz.
    (B) 8 fl oz.
    (C) 4 fl oz.
    (D) 16 fl oz.

12. How many meters are there in 16 kilometers? Circle the correct answer choice.

Ⓐ 1.6 m
Ⓑ 1,600 m
Ⓒ 16,000 m
Ⓓ 160 m

13. Use the chart provided to fill in the missing values in the table below.

1 L	1000 ml
1 g	1000 mg
1 m	1000 mm

3	L		ml
	g	5000	mg
	m	8000	mm
12	L		ml
20	g		mg

End of Ratios & Proportional Relationships

Chapter 2:

Ratios & Proportional Relationships

Answer Key
&
Detailed Explanations

Lesson 1: Expressing Ratios

Question No.	Answer	Detailed Explanations
1	C	First, to find the proper ratio, subtract the number of girls from the total number of students. The difference is the number of boys. $600-330 = 270$. So, the initial ratio is $\frac{270}{600}$. Then, to rewrite a ratio in its simplest terms, divide the numerator and denominator by the Greatest Common Factor (GCF). Here, the GCF is 30. 270 divided by 30 = 9 and 600 divided by 30 = 20, so, the simplest ratio is $\frac{9}{20}$.
2	D	First, find the ratio of emeralds to rubies. That ratio is $\frac{85}{119}$. To find how many pearls the sultan had, set up a proportion with the ratio of diamonds to pearls: $\frac{85}{119} = \frac{45}{x}$ Then, find the cross products of each: $85*x = 119*45$ Simplify: $85x = 5355$ Solve for x by dividing by 85 on both sides: $\frac{85x}{85} = \frac{5355}{85}$ $x = 63$
3	B	$75 + 125 = 200$. Therefore, the total number of birds is 200. The ratio of geese to total birds is 75:200. Simplify the ratio by dividing by the GCF (75,200)= 25, simplified ratio is 3:8.
4	D	There are $(7+5+2) = 14$ players in all. The ratio of redheads to the team is 2:14. Divide by the GCF of 2 to simplify the ratio to 1:7
5	C	Set up the proportion: $\frac{2}{14}=\frac{x}{126}$, $\frac{1}{7}=\frac{x}{126}$, cross multiply to get $7x = 126$, then divide by 7 and $x = 18$.
6	D	The total number of birds is $175+63 = 238$. Thus, the ratio of ducks to total birds is 175:238. To find the ratio in simplest terms, divide by the GCF(175, 238) =7. The ratio in simplest terms is 25:34.
7	A	The ratio of ducks to geese is 175:63. To find how many ducks, set up a proportion of $\frac{175}{63} = \frac{x}{4,725}$. Find the cross products: $175*4,725 = 63*x$ $826,875 = 63x$ Divide both sides by 63 $x = 13,125$
8	D	There are 3 teaspoons to each tablespoon. Thus $3 * \frac{10}{3} = 10$ teaspoons.

Question No.	Answer	Detailed Explanations
9	D	To find how many students there are in the grade, set up the proportion $\frac{6}{5} = \frac{24}{x}$. Notice that you can multiply $\frac{6}{5}$ by $\frac{4}{4}$ to make the numerator of 24. This makes the equivalent denominator 20. Add 24 + 20 to get the total number of students, or 44.
10	C	If the ratio of pencils to pens is $\frac{3}{2}$ then the ratio of pencils to pencils and pens is $\frac{3}{5}$. To find the number of pencils in a box with 30 pencils and pens, set up the proportion $\frac{3}{5} = \frac{x}{30}$. Then, multiply the first ratio by $\frac{6}{6}$ which will equal $\frac{18}{30}$. There are 18 pencils in the box.
11	A & D	Correct Response: 3:8 and 3/8 There are 3 shaded bows and a total of 8 bows in all. 3:8 is the correct way to write a ratio or it can be written $\frac{3}{8}$, which is read "3 out of 8".
12	4:5	4:5. There are 4 white stars and 5 gray stars.

13

1	2
2	4
3	6
4	8
5	10
6	12

The numbers are 3, 6, 10. The first row shows the ratio pattern, which is 1:2, which means each number in the left column is ½ of the number in the right column.

Lesson 2: Unit Rates

Question No.	Answer	Detailed Explanations
1	C	$\frac{1}{5}$ = a unit price of $0.20 per piece $\frac{.85}{4}$ = a unit price of $0.2125 per piece $\frac{.25}{2}$ = a unit price of $0.125 per piece. This is the best price per unit. $\frac{1.1}{6}$ = a unit price of $0.183 per piece.
2	C	The unit rate at Store A is $\frac{\$3.45}{5}$ =$0.69. 20 cans of beans would be $0.69*20= $13.80 The unit rate at Store C is $\frac{\$2.46}{4}$ = $0.615. 20 cans of beans would be $0.615*20=$12.30. Subtract $13.80−12.30=$1.50
3	B	284 miles divided by 58 miles per hour are how you will find how long it took Beverly to make the trip. (Distance ÷ rate = time) $\frac{284}{58}$ ≈ 4.9 hours 0.9 hours = 54 minutes (Multiply 60 by 0.9, because there are 60 minutes in an hour.) 4 hours and 54 minutes is how long it took Beverly to make the trip.
4	B	$7.55 x 10 = $75.55 $8.45 x 15 = $126.75 126.75 + 75.55 = 202.30 $\frac{202.30}{25}$ = $8.09
5	A	$\frac{15}{4}=\frac{60}{x}$, where 60 equals the number of minutes in an hour. 15 x 4 = 60, so multiply the original ratio $\frac{15}{4}$ by $\frac{4}{4}$ to get $\frac{60}{16}$, where 16 represents the miles per hour (mph) that she traveled.
6	C	Set up a ratio of distance/time. Here, the ratio would be $\frac{1.5}{2.5}$ Then, create a proportion $\frac{1.5}{2.5} = \frac{x}{60}$, where 60 represents the number of minutes in an hour. Find the cross products: 1.5*60 = 2.5*x Simplify: 90 = 2.5x, Divide each side by 2.5 we get, x = 36.
7	B	There are 16 ounces in a pound, so $\frac{\$7.52}{16}$ = 47¢
8	C	To find the cost of gas per mile: $\frac{\$62.90}{330}$ equals about $0.19 per mile. (Note: The capacity of the tank is extra information.)

Question No.	Answer	Detailed Explanations
9	D	$3.99/13 equals about $0.306 per ounce. Since there are 16 oz in a pound, multiply 16 by $0.306…, which equals about $4.91.
10	C	$26.00 ÷ (1/2) = $26.00 x 2 = $52.00 per ounce

11		

	1:10	1:5	1:50	1:20
$1.00 per 5 pounds		⬤		
50 pounds per box			⬤	
10 miles per gallon	⬤			
1 lap in 20 minutes				⬤

Correct Response: A. 1:5, One dollar is spent for every 5 pounds. B. 1:50, Per box refers to a quantity of 1 box, so there are 50 pounds in one box. C. 1:10, Per gallon refers to a quantity of 1 gallon, so every gallon supplies 10 miles. D. 1:20, It takes 20 minutes to run 1 lap.

| 12 | A, C & D | Choices (A), (C) and (D) are all correct. Choice (B) is incorrect because it takes 2 cups of flour to make 12 cupcakes. Choice (E) is incorrect because 1 bar of chocolate is needed for 12 cupcakes, so 2 bars of chocolate would be needed to make 24 cupcakes. |
| 13 | $ 0.40 | The bag shown in the picture consists of 8 apples. To determine the unit rate for the cost of one apple, divide the cost of all the apples by the total number of apples: $3.20 ÷ 8 = .40 So, one apple has a unit rate cost of $.40. |

Lesson 3: Solving Real World Ratio Problems

Question No.	Answer	Detailed Explanations
1	D	1000 grams/1 kilogram = 375 grams/x kilograms 1000x = 375 Divide each side by 1000 x = 0.375 kilograms
2	D	36 inches equal 1 yard, so 72 inches must equal 2 yards.
3	B	is/of = %/100 so: $\frac{x}{120} = \frac{50}{100}$ 100*x = 120*50 100x = 6000 Divide both sides by 100 x = 60
4	D	Since every foot = 12 inches, then 6 feet must equal 72 inches (6*12). Add extra 6 inches to 72 inches which is equal to 78 inches.
5	B	Divide a percentage by 100 to make an equivalent decimal form 7.5/100 = .075
6	D	is/of = %/100 $\frac{x}{60} = \frac{30}{100}$ x*100 = 60*30 100x = 1800 Divide both sides by 100 x = $18 Subtract $18 from $60. $60−$18 = $42
7	C	$\frac{6}{10} = \frac{x}{1000}$ x*10 = 6*1000 10x = 6000 Divide both sides by 10 x = 600
8	C	is/of = %/100 $\frac{34.00}{51.00} = \frac{x}{100}$ 34.00*100 = 51*x 3400 = 51x Divide both sides by 51 x = 66.67% This is the amount left to pay. 100% − 66.67% = 33.33% This is the amount the shirt was reduced by.

Question No.	Answer	Detailed Explanations
9	C	is/of = %/100 $\dfrac{x}{\$4.00} = \dfrac{28}{100}$ 4*28 = 100*x 112 = 100x Divide both sides by 100 x = $1.12 Then, multiply $1.12 * 12 = $13.44
10	A	is/of = x/100 use hours as your proportional rate 45 minutes + 45 minutes = 90 minutes or 1.5 hours $\dfrac{1.5}{24} = \dfrac{x}{100}$ 1.5*100 = 24*x 150 = 24x Divide both sides by 24 x = 6.25%
11	C	$\dfrac{is}{of} = \dfrac{\%}{100}$ $\dfrac{222}{x} = \dfrac{75}{100}$ 222 × 100 = 75 × x 22200 = 75x Divide both sides by 75 **x = 296**
12	A & C	A. $\dfrac{4}{6} = \dfrac{2}{3}$ & C. $\dfrac{6}{9} = \dfrac{2}{3}$ The ratio of grape to apple is 2:3 or $\dfrac{2}{3}$. By fractions equivalent to $\dfrac{2}{3}$, you can determine the correct ratio for the recipe.

Question 13

Feet	Yards
3	1
6	**2**
9	3
15	5
24	**8**

1 yard = 3 feet
Set up the proportion: yard/feet
(1) Let x be the number of yards in 6 feet.
$\dfrac{1}{3} = \dfrac{x}{6}$
3x = 1 x 6 = 6
x = $\dfrac{6}{3}$ = 2 yards
(2) Let y be the number of feet in 3 yards
$\dfrac{1}{3} = \dfrac{3}{y}$
1 x y = 3 x 3 = 9 or y = 9
(3) Let z be the number of yards in 24 feet.
$\dfrac{1}{3} = \dfrac{z}{24}$
3z = 1 x 24 = 24
z = $\dfrac{24}{3}$ = 8

Lesson 4: Solving Unit Rate Problems

Question No.	Answer	Detailed Explanations
1	C	Find the unit rate for one juice pouch. $\dfrac{\$6.00}{12} = \dfrac{x}{1}$ 6*1=12*x 6 = 12x Divide both sides by 12 x = $0.50 per pouch
2	B	Find the unit rate for one gallon of gas. $\dfrac{128}{4} = \dfrac{x}{1}$ 128*1=4*x 128 = 4x Divide both sides by 4 x = 32 miles per gallon
3	D	Find the unit rate for one mile. $\dfrac{39}{6} = \dfrac{x}{1}$ 39*1=6*x 39 = 6x Divide both sides by 6 x = 6.5 or 6 minutes 30 seconds
4	A	Find the unit rate for one day. $\dfrac{114}{3} = \dfrac{x}{1}$ 114*1=3*x 114 = 3x Divide both sides by 3 x = 38 laps per day
5	C	The cost of the seven items plus $15.00 should equal $65.00. If the average cost per item is x, then 7x is the cost of all seven items. Therefore 7x + $15.00 = $65.00 can be used to find x.
6	B	Find the unit rate for one day. Geoff shot 150 arrows ($15*10) $\dfrac{150}{5}$ days $= \dfrac{x}{1}$ 150*1=5*x 150 = 5x Divide both sides by 5 x = 30 arrows per day

Question No.	Answer	Detailed Explanations
7	C	Find the total number of cookies and divide by 7. The total number of cookies is 74 + 3 = 77. The number of batches is 7. So the total number of cookies per batch can be found using the expression (74 + 3)/7.
8	B	Find the unit rate for one paper. Change hours to minutes or 3 hrs = 3*60 mins $\frac{180}{124} = \frac{x}{1}$ 180*1=124*x 180 = 124x Divide both sides by 124 x = 1.45 minutes or 1 minutes and 27 seconds
9	C	Find the unit rate for both and compare. Fink's: 462 miles/21 gallons = 22 miles per gallon Conrad's: 456 miles/12 gallons = 38 gallons Difference: 38 – 22 = 16 gallons
10	D	Find the unit rate for both and compare. Myka: $4.00/30 cards = $0.13 per card Chuck: $12.00/100 cards = $0.12 per card Chuck paid 12 cents per card and Myka paid 13 cents per card. So Chuck got the better deal.
11	5	Since 3 cheeseburgers cost $15, when you divide $15 by 3, you get cost of one cheeseburger, which is $5.

12

Day	Total Money Earned $	Yards Mowed
Monday	50	2
Wednesday	75	3
Friday	25	1
Saturday	125	5

Tommy mowed 2 yards and made $50, you divide the money earned by the yards mowed, 50/2 = $ 25 per yard. Multiply each yard by $25 to calculate how much money he earned each day.

13

	$150	$10	$100	$200
10			✓	
15	✓			
20				✓
1		✓		

10 tickets sold = $100. 15 tickets sold = $150. 20 tickets sold = $200. 1 ticket sold = $10.

Lesson 5: Finding Percent

Question No.	Answer	Detailed Explanations
1	B	is/of = %/100 $\dfrac{x}{24} = \dfrac{25}{100}$ x*100 = 24*25 100x = 600 Divide both sides by 100 x = 6
2	A	is/of = %/100 $\dfrac{x}{60} = \dfrac{15}{100}$ x*100 = 60*15 100x = 900 Divide both sides by 100 x = 9
3	C	is/of = %/100 $\dfrac{9}{72} = \dfrac{x}{100}$ 9*100 = 72*x 900 = 72x Divide both sides by 72 x = 12.5%
4	B	is/of = %/100 $\dfrac{x}{190} = \dfrac{30}{100}$ x*100 = 190*30 100x = 5,700 Divide both sides by 100 x = 57
5	C	is/of = %/100 $\dfrac{x}{280} = \dfrac{15}{100}$ x*100 = 280*15 100x = 4,200 Divide both sides by 100 x = 42 cards
6	A	is/of = %/100 $\dfrac{8}{x} = \dfrac{80}{100}$ 8*100 = x*80 800 = 80x Divide both sides by 80 x = 10 gallons

Question No.	Answer	Detailed Explanations
7	B	156 of 178 legos in percentage would be $\dfrac{156}{678}$ x 100 = 23%
8	D	is/of = %/100 is the same as of/is = 100/% Is = 8; of = 15 ; % = x Substitute these values to get: $\dfrac{15}{8} = \dfrac{100}{x}$
9	B	32% of the 78 flowers are roses. Therefore, number of roses $= \dfrac{32}{100}$ x 78 = 24.96 which is approximately 25.
10	C	Total number of sheets used = 6 + 8 + 10 = 24 which is 30% of the total sheets (x). $\dfrac{30}{100}$ * X = 24 x = 80. The number of sheet not taken out is 80−24 = 56.

Question 11:

Item Purchased	Original Price	Amount of Discount	Amount Paid
Video Game	$80	20%	**$64**
Movie Ticket	$14	**20%**	$11.20
Laptop	$1,000	**25%**	$750
Shoes	$55.00	10%	$49.5

Amount paid for video game = $64, Because $80 x 0.80 = $64 (20% discount means, one has to pay 80% of the original price. 80% = 0.80)

(2) Original price of the movie ticket = $14
Amount paid = $ 11.2
Discount = 14 - 11.2 = 2.8
% Discount /100 = Discount / original price
% Discount = 100 x (Discount / original price) = 100 x ($\frac{2.8}{14}$) = $\frac{280}{14}$
= 20%

(3) Discount for the Laptop = 1000 - 750 = 250
% Discount = 100 x (Discount / original price) = 100 x ($\frac{250}{1000}$)
= $\frac{25000}{1000}$ = 25%

12	A & D	The correct answer options are A and D. Option A. $90 x .25 = $22.50 Option D. $560 x .25 = $140.00

Lesson 6: Measurement Conversion

Question No.	Answer	Detailed Explanations
1	B	There are 12 inches in a foot. $69 \text{ inches} * (\frac{1 \text{ foot}}{12 \text{ inches}}) = \frac{69}{12} = 5.75 \text{ feet}$
2	D	There are 4 quarts to a gallon. $7*4 = 28$ quarts $28 + 3 = 31$ quarts
3	D	There are 100 cm in a meter and 1000 meters in a kilometer. $3.7 \text{ km} * (\frac{1000 \text{ m}}{1 \text{ km}}) * (\frac{100 \text{ cm}}{1 \text{ m}}) = 370,000 \text{ cm}$
4	B	There are 16 ounces per pound. $136 \text{ ounces} * (\frac{1 \text{ lb}}{16 \text{ oz}}) = 8.5 \text{ pounds}$
5	C	There are 8 ounces per cup, 2 cups per pint, 2 pints per quart and 4 quarts per gallon. $5 \text{ gal} * (\frac{4 \text{ qts}}{1 \text{ gal}}) * (\frac{2 \text{ pints}}{1 \text{ qt}}) * (\frac{2 \text{ cups}}{1 \text{ pt}}) * (\frac{8 \text{ oz}}{1 \text{ cup}}) = 640 \text{ ounces}$
6	B	Find the total length of the race in meters: $1284 + 1635 + 1473 = 4392$ meters There are 1000 meters in 1 kilometer. $4392 \text{ m} * (\frac{1 \text{ km}}{1000 \text{ m}}) = 4.392 = 4.4 \text{ km}$
7	C	Find the total number of minutes for the month: $1 \text{ h } 3 \text{ m} + 1 \text{ h } 18 \text{ m} + 55 \text{ m} + 68 \text{ m} = 63 \text{ m} + 78 \text{ m} + 55 \text{ m} + 68 \text{ m} = 264$ minutes. There are 60 minutes in 1 hour. $264 \text{ min} * (\frac{1 \text{ hr}}{60 \text{ min}}) = 4.4 \text{ hours}$
8	C	There are 60 minutes in 1 hour. 3 miles/18 minutes = x miles/60 minutes $3*60 = 18*x$ $180 = 18x$ Divide both side by 18 $x = 10$ miles per hour
9	B	Find the perimeter by adding all four sides of the garden: $67 + 67 + 92 + 92 = 318$ in There are 12 inches in a foot. $318 \text{ in} * (\frac{1 \text{ foot}}{12 \text{ in}}) = 26.5 \text{ feet}$

Question No.	Answer	Detailed Explanations
10	B	There are 100 cm in a meter and 2.54 cm in 1 inch. 1.27 meters * $(\frac{100\ cm}{1\ m})$ * $(\frac{1\ in}{2.54\ cm})$ = 50 inches 50 in / 12 in = 4.17 feet = 4 feet 2 inches
11	B	8 fl oz = 1 cup
12	C	1000 meters/1 kilometer = x meters/16 kilometers 1000*16 = 1*x x = 16,000

13					
		1	3 L	**3000 ml**	Because 3 x 1000 =3000
		2	**5 g**	5000 mg	Because 5000 ÷ 1000 = 5
		3	**8 m**	8000 mm	Because 8000 ÷ 1000 = 8
		4	12 L	**12,000 ml**	Because 12 x 1000 =12,000
		5	20 g	**20,000 mg**	Because 20 x 1000=20,000

Chapter 3:
The Number System

Lesson 1: Division of Fractions

You can scan the QR code given below or use the url to access additional EdSearch resources including videos and mobile apps related to *Division of Fractions*.

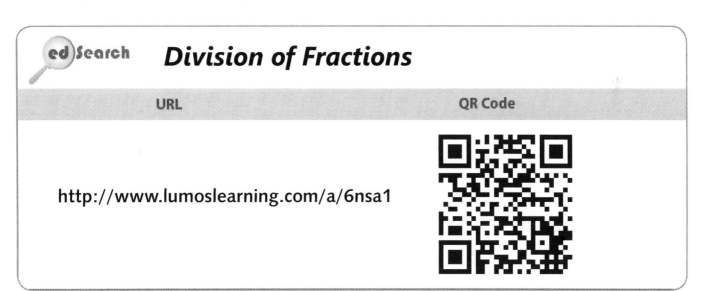

URL	QR Code
http://www.lumoslearning.com/a/6nsa1	

1. **What is the quotient of 20 divided by one-fourth?**

   Ⓐ 80
   Ⓑ 24
   Ⓒ 5
   Ⓓ 15

2. **Calculate:** $1\dfrac{1}{2} \div \dfrac{3}{4} =$

   Ⓐ 4

   Ⓑ $\dfrac{1}{2}$

   Ⓒ $\dfrac{3}{4}$

   Ⓓ 2

3. **Calculate:** $3\dfrac{2}{3} \div 2\dfrac{1}{6} =$

   Ⓐ $\dfrac{8}{13}$

   Ⓑ $\dfrac{12}{13}$

   Ⓒ $1\dfrac{5}{13}$

   Ⓓ $1\dfrac{9}{13}$

4. **Calculate:** $2\dfrac{3}{4} \div \dfrac{11}{4} =$

   Ⓐ 1
   Ⓑ 2
   Ⓒ 3
   Ⓓ 4

5. **Calculate:** $\dfrac{7}{8} \div \dfrac{3}{4} =$

Ⓐ $1\dfrac{1}{6}$

Ⓑ 2

Ⓒ $\dfrac{21}{32}$

Ⓓ $\dfrac{5}{9}$

6. **Calculate:** $6\dfrac{3}{4} \div 1\dfrac{1}{8} =$

Ⓐ $\dfrac{1}{6}$

Ⓑ 4

Ⓒ $5\dfrac{3}{4}$

Ⓓ 6

7. **Complete the following division using mental math.**

7 divided by $\dfrac{1}{5}$

Ⓐ 35

Ⓑ $\dfrac{7}{5}$

Ⓒ $\dfrac{5}{7}$

Ⓓ $\dfrac{1}{35}$

8. **Complete the following division using mental math.**

11 divided by $\dfrac{6}{6}$

Ⓐ $\dfrac{66}{66}$

Ⓑ $\dfrac{1}{11}$

Ⓒ 1

Ⓓ 11

9. **What is the result when a fraction is multiplied by its reciprocal?**

Ⓐ $\dfrac{1}{2}$

Ⓑ 10

Ⓒ 1

Ⓓ It cannot be determined.

10. **Simplify the following problem. Do not solve.**

$$\dfrac{14}{21} \div \dfrac{28}{7}$$

Ⓐ $\dfrac{14}{21} \div \dfrac{28}{7}$

Ⓑ $\dfrac{2}{3} \times \dfrac{1}{4}$

Ⓒ 1

Ⓓ 10

11. Which of the following is equal to 1 ÷ $\frac{3}{4}$? Circle the correct answer choice.

   Ⓐ $\frac{4}{3}$

   Ⓑ $\frac{2}{4}$

   Ⓒ $\frac{1}{3}$

12. Fill in the blank.

   $\frac{1}{2}$ ÷ 4 = ___?

13. Which of the following is equal to $\frac{7}{2}$ ÷ $\frac{2}{6}$? Circle the correct answer choice.

   Ⓐ $\frac{9}{2}$

   Ⓑ $\frac{5}{4}$

   Ⓒ $\frac{42}{4}$

Chapter 3

Lesson 2: Division of Whole Numbers

You can scan the QR code given below or use the url to access additional EdSearch resources including videos and mobile apps related to *Division of Whole Numbers.*

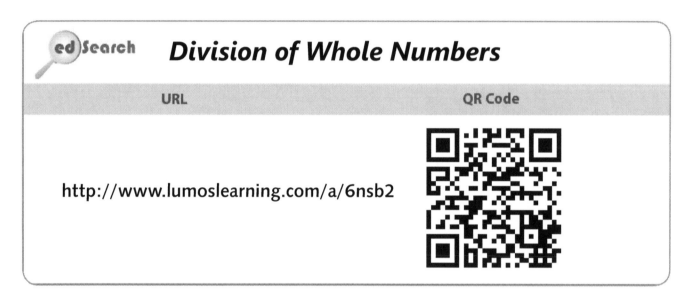

ed Search	**Division of Whole Numbers**
URL	QR Code
http://www.lumoslearning.com/a/6nsb2	

1. **A team of 12 players got an award of $1,800 for winning a championship football game. If the captain of the team is allowed to keep $315, how much money would each of the other players get? (Assume they split it equally.)**

   Ⓐ $135
   Ⓑ $125
   Ⓒ $150
   Ⓓ $123.75

2. **Peter gets a salary of $125 per week. He wants to buy a new television that costs $3,960. If he saves $55 per week, which of the following expressions could he use to figure out how many weeks it will take him to save up enough money to buy the new TV?**

   Ⓐ $3,960 ÷ ($125 − $55)
   Ⓑ $3,960 − ($125)($55)
   Ⓒ ($3,960 ÷ $125) ÷ $55
   Ⓓ $3,960 ÷ $55

3. **An expert typist typed 9,000 words in two hours. How many words per minute did she type?**

   Ⓐ 4,500 words per minute
   Ⓑ 150 words per minute
   Ⓒ 75 words per minute
   Ⓓ 38 words per minute

4. **Bethany cut off 18 inches of her hair for "Locks of Love". (Locks of Love is a non profit organization that provides wigs to people who have lost their hair due to chemotherapy.) It took her 3 years to grow it back. How much did her hair grow each month?**

   Ⓐ 1 inch
   Ⓑ 2 inches
   Ⓒ 0.25 inches
   Ⓓ 0.5 inches

5. **On "Jeopardy," during the month of September, the champions won a total of $694,562. Assuming that there were 22 "Jeopardy" shows in September, what was the average amount won each day by the champions?**

   Ⓐ $12,435
   Ⓑ $21,891
   Ⓒ $35,176
   Ⓓ $31,571

6. **A marching band wants to raise $20,000 at its annual fundraiser. If they sell tickets for $20 a piece, how many tickets will they have to sell?**

   Ⓐ 500
   Ⓑ 10,000
   Ⓒ 100
   Ⓓ 1,000

7. **A classroom needs 3,200 paper clips for a project. If there are 200 paper clips in a package, how many packages will they need in all?**

   Ⓐ 160
   Ⓑ 1,600
   Ⓒ 18
   Ⓓ 16

8. **A homebuilder is putting new shelves in each closet he is building. He has 2,592 shelves in his inventory. If each closet needs 108 shelves, how many closets can he build?**

   Ⓐ 2.4
   Ⓑ 108
   Ⓒ 42
   Ⓓ 24

9. **A toy maker needs to make $17,235 per month to meet his costs. Each toy sells for $45. How many toys does he need to sell in order to break even (cover his costs)?**

   Ⓐ 393
   Ⓑ 473
   Ⓒ 373
   Ⓓ 383

10. **A stamp collector collected 4,224 stamps last year. He collected the same amount each month. How many stamps did he collect each month?**

    Ⓐ 422
    Ⓑ 352
    Ⓒ 362
    Ⓓ 252

11. Fill in the blank

40,950 ÷ _____ = 26

12. Fill in the blank

455 ÷ _____ = 7

Chapter 3

Lesson 3: Operations with Decimals

You can scan the QR code given below or use the url to access additional EdSearch resources including videos and mobile apps related to *Operations with Decimals*.

ed Search   **Operations with Decimals**

URL	QR Code
http://www.lumoslearning.com/a/6nsb3	

1. Three friends went out to lunch together. Ben got a meal that cost $7.25, Frank got a meal that cost $8.16, and Herman got a meal that cost $5.44. If they split the check evenly, how much did they each pay for lunch? (Assume no tax)

   Ⓐ $6.95
   Ⓑ $7.75
   Ⓒ $7.15
   Ⓓ $6.55

2. Which of these is the standard form of twenty and sixty-three thousandths?

   Ⓐ 20.63000
   Ⓑ 20.0063
   Ⓒ 20.63
   Ⓓ 20.063

3. Mr. Zito bought a bicycle for $160. He spent $12.50 on repair charges. If he sold the same bicycle for $215, what would his profit be on the investment?

   Ⓐ $ 147.50
   Ⓑ $ 42.50
   Ⓒ $ 67.50
   Ⓓ $ 55.00

4. A certain book is sold in a paperback version for $4.75 or in a hardcover version for $11.50. If a copy of the book is being purchased for each of the twenty students in Mrs. Jackson's class, how much money altogether would be saved by buying the paperback version, as opposed to the hardcover version?

   Ⓐ $ 155.00
   Ⓑ $ 135.00
   Ⓒ $ 115.00
   Ⓓ $ 145.00

5. **Which of these sets contains all equivalent numbers?**

Ⓐ $\left\{0.75, \dfrac{3}{4}, 75\%, \dfrac{8}{12}\right\}$

Ⓑ $\left\{0.100, \dfrac{5}{50}, 15\%, 0.010\right\}$

Ⓒ $\left\{\dfrac{3}{8}, 35\%, 0.35, \dfrac{35}{100}\right\}$

Ⓓ $\left\{\dfrac{9}{25}, 36\%, 0.360, \dfrac{18}{50}\right\}$

6. **Brian is mowing his lawn. He and his family have 7.84 acres. Brian mows 1.29 acres on Monday, 0.85 acres on Tuesday, and 3.63 acres on Thursday. How many acres does Brian have left to mow?**

Ⓐ 2.70
Ⓑ 20.7
Ⓒ 2.07
Ⓓ 0.207

7. **Hector is planting his garden. He makes it 5.8 feet wide and 17.2 feet long. What is the area of Hector's garden?**

Ⓐ 9.976 square feet
Ⓑ 99.76 square feet
Ⓒ 99.76 feet
Ⓓ 997.6 square feet

8. **Chris and 2 of his friends go apple picking. Together they pick a bushel of apples that weighs 28.2 pounds. If Chris and his friends split the bushel of apples evenly among themselves, how many pounds of apples will each person take home?**

Ⓐ 9.4 pounds
Ⓑ 0.94 pounds
Ⓒ 94 pounds
Ⓓ 0.094 pounds

9. Joann and John are hiking over a three-day weekend. They have a total of 67.8 miles that they are planning on hiking. On Friday, they hike half of the miles. On Saturday, they hike another 20 miles. How many miles do they have left to hike on Sunday?

Ⓐ 1.39 miles
Ⓑ 31.9 miles
Ⓒ 13.9 miles
Ⓓ 139 miles

10. Margaret, Justin, and Leigh are babysitting for the neighbor's children during the summer. Each week they make a total of $72.00, and they split the money evenly. At the end of 4 weeks, how much money did Justin make?

Ⓐ $130.00
Ⓑ $144.00
Ⓒ $72.00
Ⓓ $96.00

11. Match the equation with the correct answer.

	18.711	1871.1	187.11
62.37 x 30 =			
6.237 x 30 =			
0.6237 x 30 =			

12. Fill in the blank.

7.1 × 3.2 = _____

13. Match the equation with the correct answer.

	6.67	88.84	910.54
9.13 – 2.46 =			
913 – 2.46 =			
91.3 – 2.46 =			

Chapter 3

Lesson 4: Using Common Factors

You can scan the QR code given below or use the url to access additional EdSearch resources including videos and mobile apps related to *Using Common Factors*.

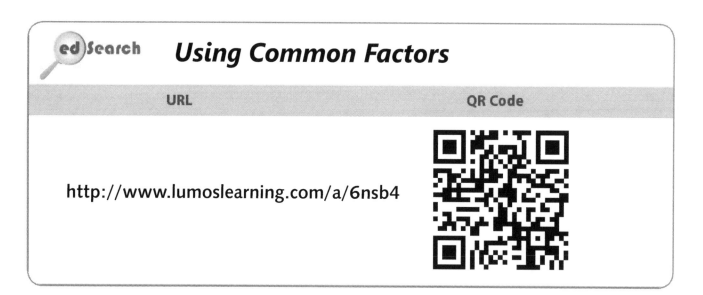

ed)Search

Using Common Factors

URL	QR Code
http://www.lumoslearning.com/a/6nsb4	

1. **Which of these statements is true of the number 17?**

   Ⓐ It is a factor of 17.
   Ⓑ It is a multiple of 17.
   Ⓒ It is prime.
   Ⓓ All of the above are true.

2. **What are the single digit prime numbers?**

   Ⓐ 2, 3, 5, and 7
   Ⓑ 1, 2, 3, 5, and 7
   Ⓒ 3, 5, and 7
   Ⓓ 1, 3, 5, and 7

3. **Which of the following sets below contains only prime numbers?**

   Ⓐ 7, 11, 49
   Ⓑ 7, 37, 51
   Ⓒ 7, 23, 47
   Ⓓ 2, 29, 93

4. **The product of three numbers is equal to 105. If the first two numbers are 7 and 5, what is the third number?**

   Ⓐ 35
   Ⓑ 7
   Ⓒ 5
   Ⓓ 3

5. **What is the prime factorization of 240?**

   Ⓐ 2 × 2 × 2 × 5
   Ⓑ 2 × 2 × 2 × 2 × 15
   Ⓒ 2 × 2 × 2 × 2 × 5 × 3
   Ⓓ 2 × 2 × 2 × 5 × 3

6. **Office A's building complex and the school building next door have the same number of rooms. Office A's building complex has floors with 5 one-room offices on each, and the school building has 11 classrooms on each floor. What is the fewest number of rooms that each building can have?**

   Ⓐ 16
   Ⓑ 6
   Ⓒ 55
   Ⓓ $\frac{5}{11}$

7. **How do you know if a number is divisible by 3?**

   Ⓐ if the ones digit is an even number
   Ⓑ if the ones digit is 0 or 5
   Ⓒ if the sum of the digits in the number is divisible by 3 or a multiple of 3
   Ⓓ if the sum of the digits in the number is divisible by 2 and 3

8. **Find the Greatest Common Factor (GCF) for 42 and 56.**

   Ⓐ 21
   Ⓑ 14
   Ⓒ 7
   Ⓓ 2

9. **What is the prime factorization of 110?**

   Ⓐ 10 × 11
   Ⓑ 110 × 1
   Ⓒ 55 × 2
   Ⓓ 2 × 5 × 11

10. **What is the LCM of 16 and 24?**

    Ⓐ 16
    Ⓑ 24
    Ⓒ 36
    Ⓓ 48

11. **Fill in the blank.**

    The Greatest Common Factor (GCF) of 24, 36, and 48 is _____.

12. **List all the factors of 20.**

13. Circle the common factors between 10 and 15.

    Ⓐ 1, 5

    Ⓑ 1, 2, 5

    Ⓒ 1, 3, 4

14. What are the common factors of 8 and 12? Write your answer in the box below.

Chapter 3

Lesson 5: Positive and Negative Numbers

You can scan the QR code given below or use the url to access additional EdSearch resources including videos and mobile apps related to *Positive and Negative Numbers*.

 ## *Positive and Negative Numbers*

URL	QR Code
http://www.lumoslearning.com/a/6nsc5	

1. Larissa has $4\frac{1}{2}$ cups of flour. She is making cookies using a recipe that calls for $2\frac{3}{4}$ cups of flour. After baking the cookies how much flour will be left?

   Ⓐ $2\frac{3}{4}$ cups

   Ⓑ $2\frac{1}{4}$ cups

   Ⓒ $2\frac{3}{8}$ cups

   Ⓓ $1\frac{3}{4}$ cups

2. The accounting ledger for the high school band showed a balance of $2,123. They purchased new uniforms for a total of $2,400. How much must they deposit into their account in order to prevent it from being overdrawn?

   Ⓐ $382
   Ⓑ $462
   Ⓒ $4,000
   Ⓓ $277

3. Juan is climbing a ladder. He begins on the first rung, climbs up four rungs, but then slides down two rungs. What rung is Juan on?

   Ⓐ 2
   Ⓑ 3
   Ⓒ 4
   Ⓓ 5

4. If last year Julie's net profit was $26,247 after she spent $14,256 on expenses, what was her gross revenue?

   Ⓐ −$40,503
   Ⓑ −$11,991
   Ⓒ $40, 503
   Ⓓ $11,991

5. The amount of snow on the ground increased by 4 inches between 4 p.m. and 6 p.m. If there was 6 inches of snow on the ground at 4 p.m. how many inches were on the ground at 6 p.m.?

   Ⓐ 10 inches
   Ⓑ 14 inches
   Ⓒ 2 inches
   Ⓓ 18 inches

6. The temperature at noon was 20° F. For the next 5 hours it dropped 2° F per hour. What was the temperature at 5:00 p.m.?

   Ⓐ 15 degrees
   Ⓑ 10 degrees
   Ⓒ 5 degrees
   Ⓓ 0 degrees

7. Tom enters an elevator that is in the basement, one floor below ground level. He travels three floors down to the parking level and then 4 floors back up. What floor does he end up on?

   Ⓐ ground level
   Ⓑ 2nd floor
   Ⓒ 3rd floor
   Ⓓ basement

8. Which of these numbers would not be found between 6 and 7 on a number line?

   Ⓐ $\dfrac{43}{6}$

   Ⓑ $\dfrac{34}{5}$

   Ⓒ $\dfrac{19}{3}$

   Ⓓ $\dfrac{100}{16}$

9. **Stacey lives on a cliff. She lives 652 feet above sea level. When she travels to town, she travels down 491 feet. What elevation is town?**

　　Ⓐ 261 feet above sea level
　　Ⓑ 161 feet below sea level
　　Ⓒ 161 feet above sea level
　　Ⓓ 141 feet above sea level

10. **Chris lives in Alaska. When he wakes up, the temperature is −53 degrees. By noon, the temperature has risen 27 degrees. What is the temperature at noon?**

　　Ⓐ −27 degrees
　　Ⓑ −26 degrees
　　Ⓒ 26 degrees
　　Ⓓ −24 degrees

11. **Which of the following would result in a negative answer? Choose all that apply.**

　　Ⓐ 25 - 56
　　Ⓑ 15 + 42
　　Ⓒ -15 + 8
　　Ⓓ -25 – 7
　　Ⓔ 74 – 32

12. **On a number line, how far apart are -27 and 30? Write your answer in the box below.**

13. **Which among the following has the lowest value?**

　　-15, 0, 10, 25

　　Enter your answer in the box below.

Chapter 3

Lesson 6: Representing Negative Numbers

You can scan the QR code given below or use the url to access additional EdSearch resources including videos and mobile apps related to *Representing Negative Numbers*.

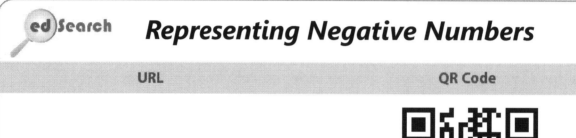

ed Search   *Representing Negative Numbers*

URL	QR Code
http://www.lumoslearning.com/a/6nsc6a	

1. **Which of these numbers would be found closest to 0 on a number line?**

   Ⓐ −5

   Ⓑ $-5\dfrac{1}{2}$

   Ⓒ $4\dfrac{1}{2}$

   Ⓓ −4

2. **On a number line, how far apart are the numbers −5.5 and 7.5?**

   Ⓐ 13 units
   Ⓑ 12 units
   Ⓒ 12.5 units
   Ⓓ 2 units

3. **Which numbers does the following number line represent?**

   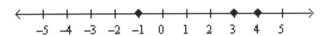

   Ⓐ {−2, 0, 5}
   Ⓑ {−3, −1, 4}
   Ⓒ {−1, 3, 5}
   Ⓓ {−1, 3, 4}

4. **If you go left on a number line, you will** _____

   Ⓐ go in a negative direction
   Ⓑ go in a positive direction
   Ⓒ increase your value
   Ⓓ none of these

5. **Which of the following numbers is NOT between −7 and −4 on the number line?**

   Ⓐ −7.2
   Ⓑ −4.8
   Ⓒ −6
   Ⓓ −5.01

6. **−7.25 is between which two numbers on the number line?**

   Ⓐ −7 and −6
   Ⓑ −5 and −3
   Ⓒ −9 and −10
   Ⓓ −7 and −8

7. **What happens when you start at any number on a number line and add its additive inverse?**

   Ⓐ The number doubles.
   Ⓑ The number halves.
   Ⓒ The sum is zero.
   Ⓓ There is no movement.

8. **Which set of numbers would be found to the left of 4 on the number line?**

   Ⓐ {−1, 4, −5}
   Ⓑ {1, −4, −5}
   Ⓒ {1, 4, −5}
   Ⓓ {1, 4, 5}

9. **On a number line, Bill places a marble on 12. He rolls the marble to the left and it moves 21 spaces and then rolls back to the right 3 spaces. What number does the marble end up on?**

   Ⓐ −21
   Ⓑ −8
   Ⓒ −9
   Ⓓ −6

10. **Which number would be found on the number line between 0 and −1?**

   Ⓐ −1.2
   Ⓑ 1.2
   Ⓒ −0.8
   Ⓓ 0.8

11. Circle the number with the highest value.

Ⓐ −17

Ⓑ −28

Ⓒ −36

12. Which number(s) have a value lower than 3? Select all that apply.

Ⓐ −5

Ⓑ 6

Ⓒ −18

Ⓓ −23

Ⓔ 4

Chapter 3

Lesson 7: Ordered Pairs

You can scan the QR code given below or use the url to access additional EdSearch resources including videos and mobile apps related to *Ordered Pairs*.

ed)Search **Ordered Pairs**

URL	QR Code
http://www.lumoslearning.com/a/6nsc6b	

1. In what Quadrant (I, II, III, IV) does the point (−12, 20) lie?

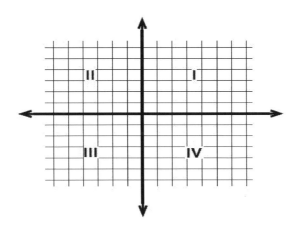

   Ⓐ Quadrant I
   Ⓑ Quadrant II
   Ⓒ Quadrant III
   Ⓓ Quadrant IV

2. In what Quadrant (I, II, III, IV) does the point (8, −9) lie?

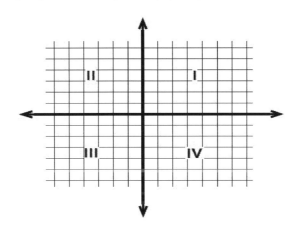

   Ⓐ Quadrant I
   Ⓑ Quadrant II
   Ⓒ Quadrant III
   Ⓓ Quadrant IV

3. In what Quadrant (I, II, III, IV) does the point (−0.75, −0.25) lie?

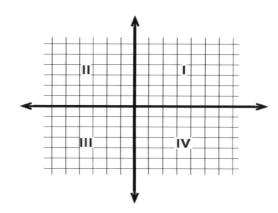

Ⓐ Quadrant I
Ⓑ Quadrant II
Ⓒ Quadrant III
Ⓓ Quadrant IV

4. Point A, located at (10,−4), is reflected across the x-axis. What are the coordinates of the reflected point?

Ⓐ (−10, −4)
Ⓑ (10, −4)
Ⓒ (10, 4)
Ⓓ (−10, 4)

5. Point B, located at (6,3), is reflected across the y-axis. What are the coordinates of the reflected point?

Ⓐ (6, 3)
Ⓑ (−6, −3)
Ⓒ (6, −3)
Ⓓ (−6, 3)

6. Point C, located at (2, 9), is reflected across the x-axis called Point C'. Point C' is then reflected across the y-axis called Point C". What are the coordinates of Point C"?

Ⓐ (−2, −9)
Ⓑ (2, 9)
Ⓒ (2, −9)
Ⓓ (−2, 9)

7. **Which Quadrant contains the most points in the following list of ordered pairs?**
    (3, 4), (−2,4), (3, −2), (4, −3), (−9, −5), (1, −3), (4, −12), (6, 14), (−5, −11), (−99, −43)

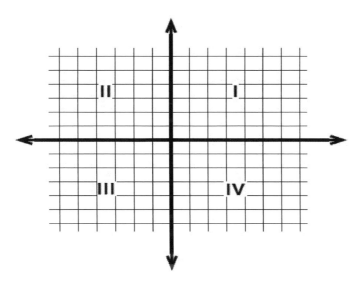

Ⓐ Quadrant I
Ⓑ Quadrant II
Ⓒ Quadrant III
Ⓓ Quadrant IV

8. **The following points have been reflected across the y-axis: (5, 1), (1, −3), (−5, 3), (−3, 1), (6, −2), (−8, 4), (7, 12). How many of the reflected points fall in Quadrant II?**

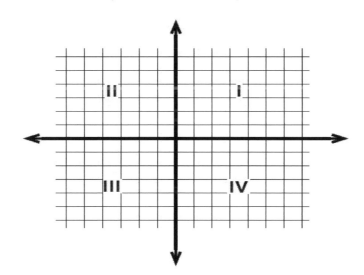

Ⓐ 0
Ⓑ 1
Ⓒ 2
Ⓓ 3

9. The following four points were reflected across the y-axis. A (4, 0), B (0, 0), C (3,0), D(−6,0). Which of the four reflected points (A', B', C', D') is not graphed properly below?

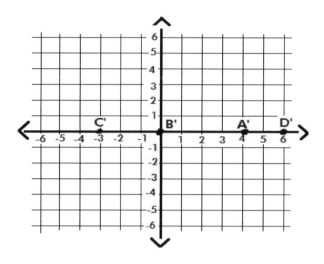

Ⓐ Point A'
Ⓑ Point B'
Ⓒ Point C'
Ⓓ Point D'

10. A point located at (12, −4) is reflected across the x-axis. In which quadrant (I, II, III, IV) will the reflected point be located?

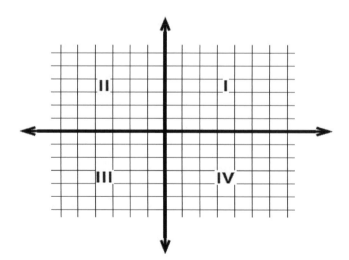

Ⓐ Quadrant I
Ⓑ Quadrant II
Ⓒ Quadrant III
Ⓓ Quadrant IV

11. Circle the correct ordered pair for the point plotted below.

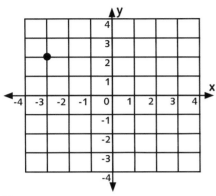

Ⓐ (3,2)
Ⓑ (-3,-2)
Ⓒ (-3,2)

12. What are the coordinates of point 'A' ? Enter your answer in the box below.

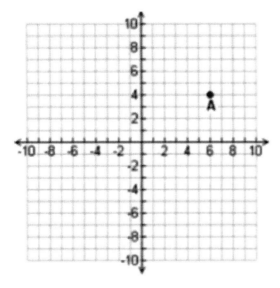

Chapter 3

Lesson 8: Number Line & Coordinate Plane

You can scan the QR code given below or use the url to access additional EdSearch resources including videos and mobile apps related to *Number Line & Coordinate Plane*.

ed)Search	**Number Line & Coordinate Plane**
URL	**QR Code**
http://www.lumoslearning.com/a/6nsc6c	

1. What number does the dot represent on the number line?

         9   16

Ⓐ 12
Ⓑ 13
Ⓒ 14
Ⓓ 15

2. What number does the dot represent on the number line?

       -5   3

Ⓐ −2
Ⓑ −1
Ⓒ 0
Ⓓ 1

3. What number does the dot represent on the number line?

      -2   14

Ⓐ 0
Ⓑ 1
Ⓒ 4
Ⓓ 6

4. What number does the dot represent on the number line?

      -10   -6

Ⓐ −5
Ⓑ −7.5
Ⓒ −8
Ⓓ −8.5

5. What number does the dot represent on the number line?

Ⓐ −5
Ⓑ 0
Ⓒ 5
Ⓓ 10

6. Select the point located at (1,−2)

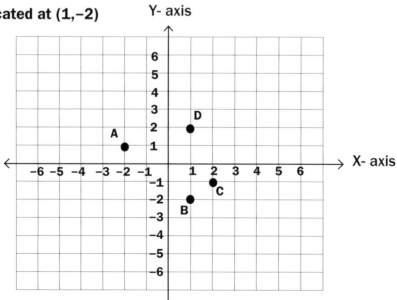

Ⓐ Point A
Ⓑ Point B
Ⓒ Point C
Ⓓ Point D

7. Select the point located at (−3,5)

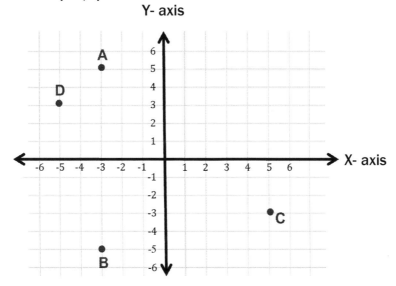

Ⓐ Point A
Ⓑ Point B
Ⓒ Point C
Ⓓ Point D

8. Select the point located at (−4,−5)

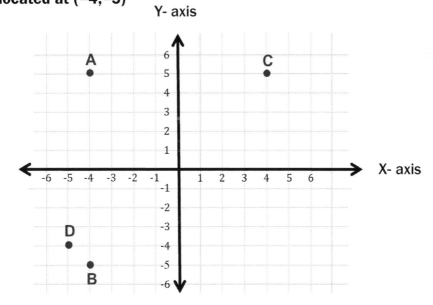

Ⓐ Point A
Ⓑ Point B
Ⓒ Point C
Ⓓ Point D

9. **Select the point located at (−1.5, 0.5)**

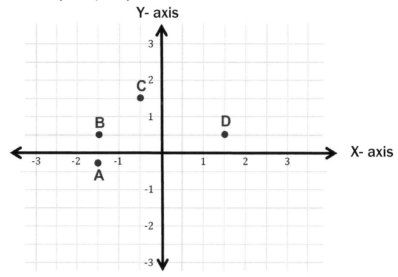

Ⓐ   Point A
Ⓑ   Point B
Ⓒ   Point C
Ⓓ   Point D

10. **Which of the following points is not graphed below? (3, 4), (−2,4), (3, 2), (−4,−3)**

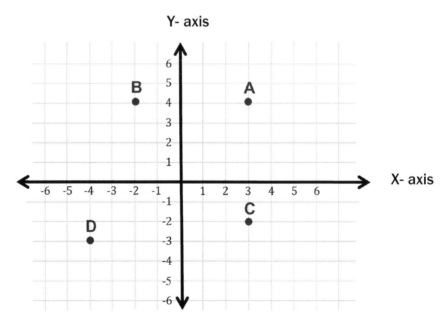

Ⓐ   (3, 4)
Ⓑ   (−2, 4)
Ⓒ   (3, 2)
Ⓓ   (−4, −3)

11. Circle the point that names the ordered pair (-9, -2).

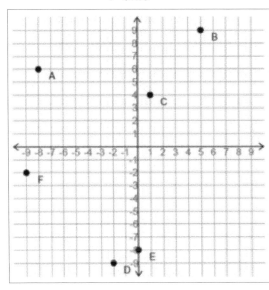

Y- axis

X- axis

Point A   Point B   Point C

Point D   Point E   Point F

12. Choose the set of numbers that are correctly ordered from least to greatest. Use the number line to help you. Choose all answers that apply.

Ⓐ 5, 2, 0, -1, -3
Ⓑ -3, -1, 0, 3, 5
Ⓒ -5, -2, 1, 4, 5
Ⓓ 0, 1, 3, -4, -5
Ⓓ None of the above

Chapter 3

Lesson 9: Absolute Value

You can scan the QR code given below or use the url to access additional EdSearch resources including videos and mobile apps related to *Absolute Value*.

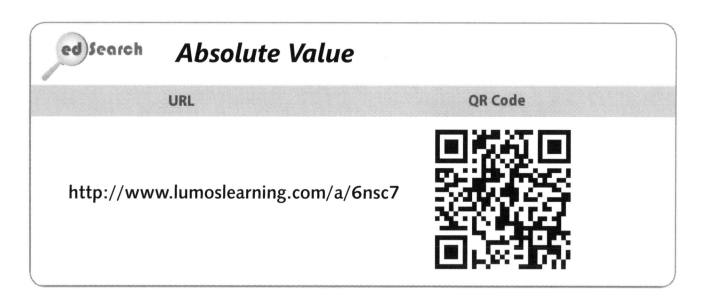

ed)Search   ***Absolute Value***

URL	QR Code
http://www.lumoslearning.com/a/6nsc7	

1. **Evaluate the following: 17 – |(7)(–3)|**

    Ⓐ 38
    Ⓑ –4
    Ⓒ 4
    Ⓓ 13

2. **Evaluate the following: 16 + |(7)(–3) – 44| – 5**

    Ⓐ 76
    Ⓑ 86
    Ⓒ 34
    Ⓓ 44

3. **Evaluate the following: |15 – 47| + 9 – |(–2)(–4) – 17|**

    Ⓐ 32
    Ⓑ –32
    Ⓒ 50
    Ⓓ 76

4. **Evaluate the following: 18 + 3 |6 – 25| – 11**

    Ⓐ 64
    Ⓑ 100
    Ⓒ 122
    Ⓓ 57

5. **Evaluate the following: 77 – |(–8)(3) + (–10)(4)|**

    Ⓐ 13
    Ⓑ 141
    Ⓒ –141
    Ⓓ –93

6. **Evaluate the following: 21 – |8 – (–5)(7)| – 54**

    Ⓐ –6
    Ⓑ 10
    Ⓒ –118
    Ⓓ –76

7. **Evaluate: |9 – 3k| = 3**

   (A) k = 0
   (B) k = 2
   (C) k = 2 or k = 4
   (D) k = −4

8. **Is the absolute value of a negative integer positive or negative?**

   (A) Positive
   (B) Negative
   (C) Neither
   (D) It depends on the magnitude of the number.

9. **What is the value of –|24|?**

   (A) 1/24
   (B) −1/24
   (C) −24
   (D) 24

10. **What is the value of |45 – 75|?**

   (A) −115
   (B) 115
   (C) 30
   (D) −30

11. **What is the value of |14| – |−28|? Write your answer in the box below.**

12. **Which is greater, |24| or |−25|? Write the answer in the box below.**

Chapter 3

Lesson 10: Rational Numbers in Context

You can scan the QR code given below or use the url to access additional EdSearch resources including videos and mobile apps related to *Rational Numbers in Context*.

edSearch	**Rational Numbers in Context**
URL	**QR Code**
http://www.lumoslearning.com/a/6nsc7b	

1. **Xavier has a golf score of –7 (We write –7 because it is 7 points below par) and Curtis has a golf score of –12. Who has the higher score?**

   Ⓐ Xavier has the higher score.
   Ⓑ Curtis has the higher score.
   Ⓒ Because both scores are below par, neither one has the higher score.
   Ⓓ We cannot tell who has the higher score because we do not know what par is.

2. **Kelly has read $\frac{5}{6}$ of a book. Helen has read $\frac{9}{12}$ of the same book. Who has read more of the book?**

   Ⓐ $\frac{5}{6}$ is more than $\frac{9}{12}$ so Kelly has read more.

   Ⓑ $\frac{5}{6}$ is less than $\frac{9}{12}$ so Helen has read more.

   Ⓒ $\frac{5}{6}$ is the same as $\frac{9}{12}$ so both Kelly and Helen have read the same amount.

   Ⓓ We cannot tell who has read more because the fractions have different denominators.

3. **The record low temperature for NY is –52°F. The record low temperature for Alaska is –80°F. Which of the following inequalities accurately compares these two temperatures?**

   Ⓐ $-52° F < -80° F$
   Ⓑ $-80° F > -52° F$
   Ⓒ $-52° F = -80° F$
   Ⓓ $-52° F > -80° F$

4. **A cake recipe calls for $1\frac{3}{4}$ cups of soy flour, $\frac{20}{8}$ cups of rice flour and 1.6 cups of wheat flour. Which of the following inequalities compares these three quantities accurately?**

   Ⓐ $1.6 < \frac{20}{8} < 1\frac{3}{4}$

   Ⓑ $\frac{20}{8} > 1\frac{3}{4} > 1.6$

   Ⓒ $\frac{20}{8} > 1\frac{3}{4} < 1.6$

   Ⓓ $1\frac{3}{4} > 1.6 > \frac{20}{8}$

5. Doug and Sissy went scuba diving. Doug descended to −143 feet and Sissy descended to −134 feet. Who dove deeper?

    Ⓐ −134 > −143, so Sissy dove deeper.
    Ⓑ −134 < −143, so Doug dove deeper.
    Ⓒ −134 = −143, so neither one dove deeper as they descended the same amount.
    Ⓓ |−143|>|−134|, so Doug dove deeper.

6. At the annual town festival $\frac{4}{15}$ of the vendors sold outdoor items, 0.4 sold clothing or indoor items and $\frac{1}{3}$ sold food. Which of the following inequalities compares these three quantities accurately?

    Ⓐ $0.4 < \frac{4}{15} < \frac{1}{3}$

    Ⓑ $\frac{4}{15} > 0.4 > \frac{1}{3}$

    Ⓒ $0.4 > \frac{1}{3} > \frac{4}{15}$

    Ⓓ $\frac{1}{3} < \frac{4}{15} < 0.4$

7. A school of fish (S1) is spotted in the ocean at 15 feet below sea level. A second school (S2) of fish is spotted at $\frac{33}{3}$ feet below sea level. A third school (S3) of fish is spotted 11.5 feet below sea level. Order these numbers from deepest to shallowest. Note: The symbol > means deeper and < means shallower

    Ⓐ S1 < S3 < S2
    Ⓑ S3 < S2 < S1
    Ⓒ S1 > S3 > S2
    Ⓓ S3 < S1 < S2

8. During the first snowfall of the year, Henderson recorded the snow fall each day. The first day $\frac{4}{5}$ of a foot fell. On the second day $\frac{5}{7}$ of a foot fell. On which day did more snow fall?

   Ⓐ $\frac{4}{5} > \frac{5}{7}$, so more snow fell on the first day.

   Ⓑ $\frac{4}{5} < \frac{5}{7}$, so more snow fell on the second day.

   Ⓒ $\frac{4}{5} = \frac{5}{7}$, so the same amount of snow fell on both days.

   Ⓓ We cannot tell from this information because the fractions have different denominators.

9. Molly has $365 in her savings account. She withdraws $415. Bill has a savings account balance of –$45. Which of the following statements is correct?

   Ⓐ Both Molly and Bill owe the bank the same amount.
   Ⓑ Molly owes the bank more than Bill.
   Ⓒ Bill owes the bank more than Molly.
   Ⓓ Neither Molly or Bill owe the bank any money.

10. Jeremiah and Farley each bought 5 boxes of energy bars. Within a week Jeremiah eats $2\frac{5}{6}$ boxes and Farley eats $1\frac{15}{9}$ boxes. Who has more left?

    Ⓐ Jeremiah has more left.
    Ⓑ Farley has more left.
    Ⓒ They both have the same amount left.
    Ⓓ We cannot tell from this information because the mixed numbers have different denominators.

11. Which temperature is hotter, 32 degrees or 56 degrees? Enter your answer in the box below.

12. Select all numbers with a value greater than -5.

    Ⓐ -17
    Ⓑ -3
    Ⓒ 25
    Ⓓ -7
    Ⓔ -100

Chapter 3

Lesson 11: Interpreting Absolute Value

You can scan the QR code given below or use the url to access additional EdSearch resources including videos and mobile apps related to *Interpreting Absolute Value*.

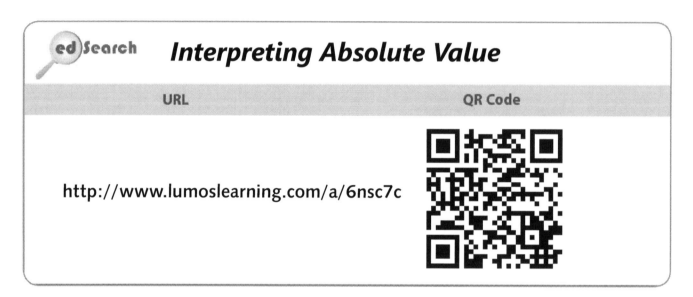

ed Search · **Interpreting Absolute Value**

URL	QR Code
http://www.lumoslearning.com/a/6nsc7c	

1. What is the absolute value of the number represented by the dot plotted below?

-7   0   8

Ⓐ −3
Ⓑ 1
Ⓒ 3
Ⓓ 4

2. What is the absolute value of the number represented by the dot plotted below?

-3   0   4

Ⓐ −2
Ⓑ −1
Ⓒ 1
Ⓓ 2

3. Which symbol will make the following a true statement? $|-27|$ _____ 19

Ⓐ >
Ⓑ <
Ⓒ =
Ⓓ ≤

4. Which symbol will make the following a true statement? −4 _____ $-|-6|$

Ⓐ >
Ⓑ <
Ⓒ =
Ⓓ ≤

5. Which of the following numbers will make both inequalities true? $-12 < x;\ |x| < 4$

Ⓐ $x = -5$
Ⓑ $x = -1$
Ⓒ $x = -7$
Ⓓ $x = -4$

6. Ruth, who lives in Florida at an elevation of 30 meters, goes on a vacation to the Grand Cayman Islands, at an elevation of 24 meters, to go scuba diving at an elevation of −30 meters. Which elevation has the greatest absolute value?

Ⓐ 30 meters
Ⓑ 24 meters
Ⓒ −30 meters
Ⓓ Both 30 meters and −30 meters have the greater absolute value.

7. Connie, Julie, and Shelley's parents have encouraged them to save their money. Connie has an account balance of $215, Julie has −$100, and Shelley has −$250. Which inequality accurately represents the relative absolute values of each account.

Ⓐ $|\$215| < |-\$100| < |-\$250|$
Ⓑ $|-\$250| < |-\$100| < |\$215|$
Ⓒ $|-\$100| > |\$215| > |-\$250|$
Ⓓ $|-\$100| < |\$215| < |-\$250|$

8. The buoys on a certain lake mark the distance in meters from a center buoy. All buoys directly south are given negative numbers and all buoys directly north are given positive numbers. Betsy is located at buoy −6.2 and her brother Luis is located at buoy 6.5. Based on this information, which one of the following statements is not true.

Ⓐ Betsy is closer to the center buoy than Luis
Ⓑ Luis is 6.5 meters from the center buoy.
Ⓒ Luis is 0.2 meters farther from the center buoy than Betsy.
Ⓓ Betsy is 12.7 meters from Luis.

9. Over the last three months Ophelia, Aaron, Nathan, and Rebecca recorded their weight. The table shows their initial and final weights.

Name	Initial Weight, lbs	Final Weight, lbs
Ophelia	145	157
Aaron	178	163
Nathan	205	217
Rebecca	136	128

Whose weight had the least absolute change?

Ⓐ Ophelia
Ⓑ Aaron
Ⓒ Nathan
Ⓓ Rebecca

10. The table below records the lowest and highest temperatures for four states.

State	Lowest Temp, °F	Highest Temp, °F
New York	−52	108
Texas	−23	120
Florida	−2	109
North Carolina	−34	110

Which state has the broadest range of temperature extremes?

Ⓐ New York
Ⓑ Texas
Ⓒ Florida
Ⓓ North Carolina

11. Sequence the numbers as they would fall on the number line in order from least to greatest. Enter the correct answers in the boxes given below.

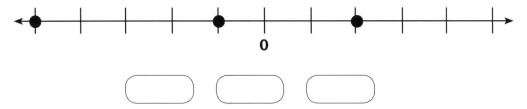

12. Sequence the numbers as they would fall on the number line in order from least to greatest. Which number highest absolute value in this number line? Enter the numbers in the correct answers in the boxes given below.

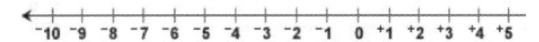

Ⓐ +4
Ⓑ -9
Ⓒ -5
Ⓓ +2
Ⓔ -10
Ⓕ -1

Chapter 3

Lesson 12: Comparisons of Absolute Value

You can scan the QR code given below or use the url to access additional EdSearch resources including videos and mobile apps related to *Comparisons of Absolute Value*.

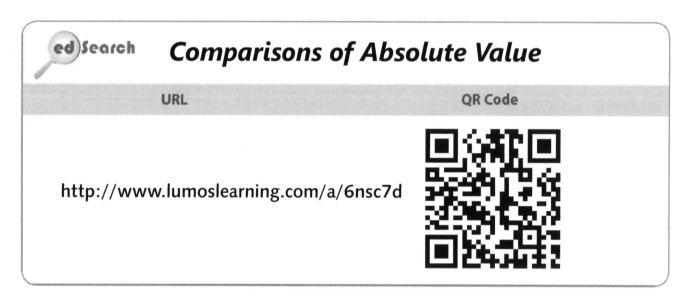

ed Search

Comparisons of Absolute Value

URL	QR Code
http://www.lumoslearning.com/a/6nsc7d	

1. **Which account balance represents the greatest debt?**
   $20, −$45, −$5, $10

   Ⓐ $20
   Ⓑ −$45
   Ⓒ −$5
   Ⓓ $10

2. **Which of the following is the warmest temperature?**
   5°F above zero, 6°F below zero, 10°F below zero, 2°F above zero

   Ⓐ 5°F above zero
   Ⓑ 6°F below zero
   Ⓒ 10°F below zero
   Ⓓ 2°F above zero

3. **Anneliese spent $58.00 on music items and paid $35.00 on a lay-away item. If she has −142.00 left in her account, how much did she start with?**

   Ⓐ $−49.00
   Ⓑ $93.00
   Ⓒ $135.00
   Ⓓ −$235.00

4. **The Murphys began their summer trip from home at an elevation of 439 feet. They drove to the mountains and climbed to an elevation of 1839 feet. After their visit on the top of the mountain, they drove down the mountainside 527 feet where they stopped for lunch. At the end of the day they spent the night at a campground at an elevation 264 feet higher than the restaurant. What is the difference in elevation between the campground and home?**

   Ⓐ 1048 feet
   Ⓑ 1137 feet
   Ⓒ 1576 feet
   Ⓓ 2012 feet

5. **Before Tonya went shopping she had $165.00 in her account. She returned a jacket that cost $46.50, bought 2 pairs of socks for $5.99 each, and went to lunch and a movie for $28.00. What is Tonya's account balance now?**

   Ⓐ $125.02
   Ⓑ $158.48
   Ⓒ $171.52
   Ⓓ $177.51

6. The Casey quadruplets live in four different states. Dominik lives in Nantucket, Massachusetts at an elevation of 28 feet; Denzel lives in New Orleans, Louisiana at an elevation of 5.3 feet below sea level; Kaila lives in California near Death Valley at an elevation of 7 feet below sea level; and Malik lives in Nome, Alaska at an elevation of 20 feet. Who lives at the lowest elevation?

Ⓐ Dominik
Ⓑ Denzel
Ⓒ Kaila
Ⓓ Malik

7. One day in January the Casey quadruplets compared their location temperature.

Location	Temperature, °C
Nome, Alaska	14.9 below zero
Nantucket, Massachusetts	5.1 below zero
New Orleans, Louisiana	6 above zero
Death Valley, California	15 above zero

Which location has the warmest temperature?

Ⓐ Nome, Alaska
Ⓑ Nantucket, Massachusetts
Ⓒ New Orleans, Louisiana
Ⓓ Death Valley, California

8. Sato, her brother Ichiro, and two friends, Aran and Mio, went to a festival. Before they could board any ride they had to be taller than the wooden height checker at each ride. At one ride Sato was 4 inches taller, Ichiro was 2 inches shorter, Aran was 6 inches taller and Mio was 2.5 inches shorter than the wooden height checker. Who is the shortest person?

Ⓐ Sato
Ⓑ Ichiro
Ⓒ Aran
Ⓓ Mio

9. Leary went to a sports store with $60.00 and bought a sweat shirt, athletic tape and baseball socks. If he received $3.72 in change, how much did his purchases cost?

Ⓐ $63.72
Ⓑ $61.18
Ⓒ $56.28
Ⓓ $47.28

10. Reilley owes $75.38 for his phone and $35.00 in dues. He expects to receive a credit of $26.16 for a wrong charge. If he currently has $629.00 in his account, what will be his account balance after all debts and credits are completed?

Ⓐ $713.22
Ⓑ $544.78
Ⓒ $518.62
Ⓓ $492.46

11. Select all numbers with an absolute value less than 20.

Ⓐ |-5|
Ⓑ |12|
Ⓒ |2|
Ⓓ |-18|
Ⓔ None of the above

12. Find the Value of |12| - |-11| = _____?

Chapter 3

Lesson 13: Coordinate Plane

You can scan the QR code given below or use the url to access additional EdSearch resources including videos and mobile apps related to *Coordinate Plane*.

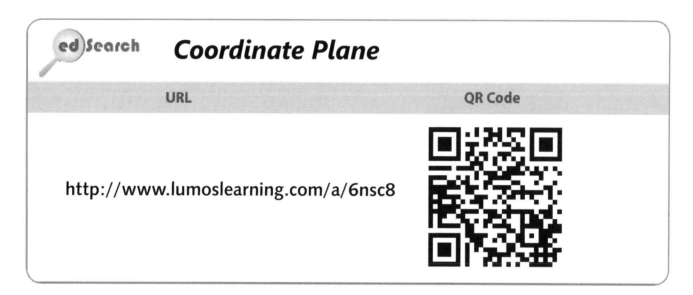

URL	QR Code
http://www.lumoslearning.com/a/6nsc8	

1. **Ricky and Becca are going hiking. Below is the map that they are using. They start out at (−3.6, −2.6). They hike four units to the east and six units to the north. What are the coordinates of their new location? (Note: North is up on this map.)**

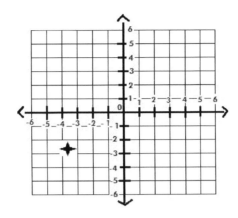

Ⓐ (0.6, 3.6)
Ⓑ (0.4, 3.4)
Ⓒ (0.4, 3.6)
Ⓓ (1.6, 3.6)

2. **The absolute value of the coordinates are (5, 8). What are the coordinates in Quadrant II?**

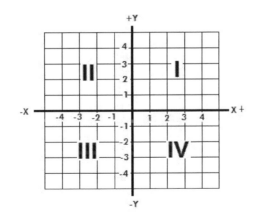

Ⓐ (−5, −8)
Ⓑ (5, −8)
Ⓒ (5, 8)
Ⓓ (−5, 8)

3. **What is the absolute value of the coordinates shown on the graph?**

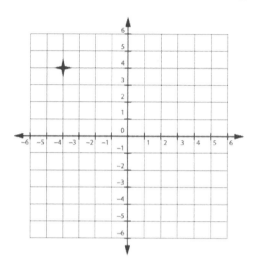

Ⓐ (−4, 4)
Ⓑ (4, 4)
Ⓒ (4, −4)
Ⓓ (−4, −4)

4. **Greg is in the jungle taking pictures of wildlife. He has to walk 5 units north and 3 units west to get back to his village. What are the coordinates of Greg's village?**
    (Note: North is up on this map. Also, consider Greg's starting position as origin)

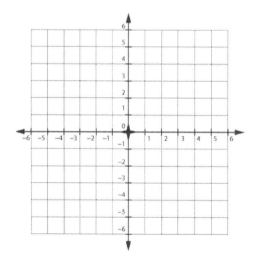

Ⓐ (−3, 5)
Ⓑ (3, 5)
Ⓒ (−3, −5)
Ⓓ (3, −5)

5. **How many units does Yolanda need to walk from point C to point D? (Note: North is up on this map.)**

Ⓐ 1 unit west and 7 units north
Ⓑ 1 unit east and 7 units south
Ⓒ 1 unit west and 7 units south
Ⓓ 7 units west and 1 unit south

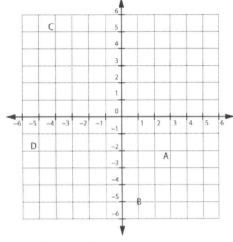

6. **What is the absolute value of Point D's coordinates?**

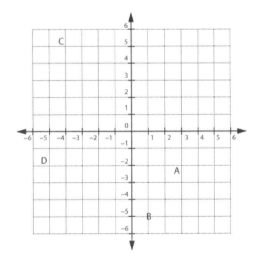

Ⓐ (−5, 2)
Ⓑ (5, −2)
Ⓒ (−5, −2)
Ⓓ (5, 2)

7. **There is a set of coordinates in Quadrant 4. The absolute value of x = 7. The absolute value of y = 3. What are the coordinates?**

Ⓐ (−7, −3)
Ⓑ (−3, −7)
Ⓒ (7, −3)
Ⓓ (−7, 3)

8. There is a set of coordinates in Quadrant 2. The absolute value of x = 3. The absolute value of y = 9. What are the coordinates?

Ⓐ (−9, −3)
Ⓑ (−3, −9)
Ⓒ (9, −3)
Ⓓ (−3, 9)

9. The graph below shows the top of a mountain. If the value y = 0 is at sea level and the y-axis is measuring altitude, how far below sea level is the point (0, −6)?

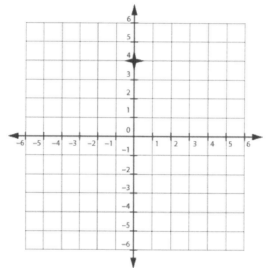

Ⓐ 10 units below sea level
Ⓑ 6 units above sea level
Ⓒ 6 units below sea level
Ⓓ 10 units above sea level

10. The coordinates (−2, 8) are in Quadrant II. If the absolute values of x and y were to stay the same, but the point was moved to Quadrant IV, what would the coordinates be?

Ⓐ (8, −2)
Ⓑ (−8, 2)
Ⓒ (−2, −8)
Ⓓ (2, −8)

11. What is the distance between these points shown in the picture? Enter the answer in the box given below.

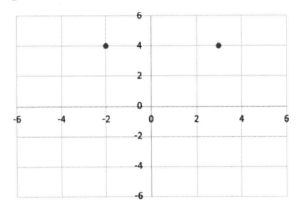

12. Which of the following ordered pairs would fall in Quadrant I on the coordinate plane? Choose all that apply.

Ⓐ (-4, 5)
Ⓑ (2, 3)
Ⓒ (2, -5)
Ⓓ (1, 1)
Ⓔ (3, 1)
Ⓕ (-3, -5)

13. Circle the point that names the ordered pair (0, -8).

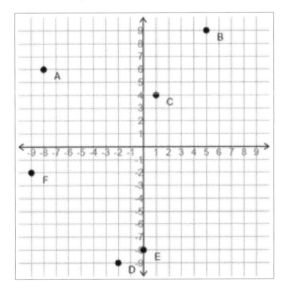

Point A Point B Point C

Point D Point E Point F

End of The Number System

Chapter 3: The Number System

Answer Key
&
Detailed Explanations

Lesson 1: Division of Fractions

Question No.	Answer	Detailed Explanations
1	A	The original problem is: $$\frac{20}{1} \div \frac{1}{4} =$$ To divide fractions, you must Keep (the first fraction), Change (the division to multiplication), and Flip (the second fraction, or, take the reciprocal). $$\frac{20}{1} \times \frac{4}{1} = \frac{80}{1} = 80$$
2	D	The original problem is: $$1\frac{1}{2} \div \frac{3}{4} =$$ First, find the improper fraction of the first mixed number (numerator = bottom times the side plus the top) = [(2*1)+1], Fraction = $\frac{3}{2}$ To divide fractions, you must keep (the first fraction), Change (the division to multiplication), Flip (the second fraction, or, take the reciprocal). $$\frac{3}{2} \times \frac{4}{3} = \frac{12}{6}$$ Simplify by factoring out the GCF of 6. The answer is $\frac{2}{1}$ or 2
3	D	The original problem is: $$3\frac{2}{3} \div 2\frac{1}{6} =$$ First, find the improper fraction of the first mixed number (numerator = bottom times the side plus the top) = [(3*3)+2], Fraction=$\frac{11}{3}$. Then, find the improper fraction of the second mixed number (numerator = bottom times the side plus the top = [(2*6)+1], Fraction = $\frac{13}{6}$ To divide fractions, you must keep (the first fraction), Change (the division to multiplication), Flip (the second fraction, or, take the reciprocal). $$\frac{11}{3} \times \frac{6}{13} = \frac{66}{39}$$ Simplify by factoring out the GCF of 3. The answer is $\frac{22}{13}$ Divide $\frac{22}{13}$ to get a mixed number: The answer is $1\frac{9}{13}$.

Question No.	Answer	Detailed Explanation
4	A	The original problem is: $2\frac{3}{4} \div \frac{11}{4} =$ First convert the mixed fraction into improper fraction by using Numerator of the improper fraction = denominator of mixed fraction x whole part of the mixed fraction + numerator of the mixed fraction whereas the denominator of the improper fraction is same as that of the mixed fraction. $2\frac{3}{4} \div \frac{11}{4} = \frac{11}{4} \div \frac{11}{4} = 1$
5	A	The original problem is: $\frac{7}{8} \div \frac{3}{4} =$ Division of fractions can be obtained by multiplying the dividend with the reciprocal of the divisor. Thus, $\frac{7}{8} \div \frac{3}{4} = \frac{7}{8} \times \frac{4}{3} = \frac{28}{24} = \frac{7}{6} = 1\frac{1}{6}$
6	D	The original problem is: $6\frac{3}{4} \div 1\frac{1}{8} =$ First convert the mixed fractions into improper fraction by using Numerator of the improper fraction = denominator of mixed fraction x whole part of the mixed fraction + numerator of the mixed fraction whereas the denominator of the improper fraction is same as that of the mixed fraction. So, $6\frac{3}{4} \div 1\frac{1}{8} = \frac{27}{4} \div \frac{8}{9}$ Division of fractions can be obtained by multiplying the dividend with the reciprocal of the divisor. Thus, $\frac{27}{4} \div \frac{9}{8} = \frac{27}{4} \times \frac{8}{9}$ Cross factor out the GCF of 4 from 4 and 8 Cross factor out the GCF of 9 from 9 and 27 $\frac{3}{1} \times \frac{2}{1} = 6$

Question No.	Answer	Detailed Explanation
7	A	To divide the fractions, you must Keep (the first fraction), Change (the division to multiplication), and Flip (the second fraction, or, take the reciprocal). The second fraction then reads $\frac{5}{1}$. Because $\frac{5}{1}$ is the same as 5, the problem simplifies to 7 X 5 = 35.
8	D	Since $\frac{6}{6}$ is equal to 1, the problem simplifies to 11 divided by 1. The answer is 11.
9	C	When any fraction is multiplied by its reciprocal, the cross numerators and denominators will always factor to 1.
10	B	$\frac{14}{21} \div \frac{28}{7}$ Becomes $\frac{14}{21} \times \frac{7}{28}$ After Keep−Change−Flip. Then, cross factor out a GCF of 7 from the 14 and 21, and a GCF of 7 from the 7 and 28. The simplified problem becomes: $\frac{2}{3} \times \frac{1}{4}$
11	A	$\frac{4}{3}$. Because $1 \div \frac{3}{4} = \frac{1}{1} \times \frac{4}{3} = \frac{4}{3}$
12	$\frac{1}{8}$	$\frac{1}{8}$. Because $\frac{1}{2} \div \frac{4}{1} = \frac{1}{2} \times \frac{1}{4} = \frac{1}{8}$
13	C	$\frac{42}{4}$. Because $\frac{7}{2} \div \frac{2}{6} = \frac{7}{2} \times \frac{6}{2} = \frac{42}{4}$

Question No.	Answer	Detailed Explanation
		Lesson 2: Division of Whole Numbers
1	A	First, find the difference of $1,800 − $315 = $1,485 Then, divide $1,485/11 = $135
2	D	To find the answer, divide $3,960 ÷ 55. (Note: The $125 is unnecessary information.)
3	C	1 hour = 60 minutes, so 2 hours = 120 minutes So, 9,000 ÷ 120 = 75
4	D	1 year = 12 months, so 3 years = 36 months 18 ÷ 36 =0.5 inches per month.
5	D	Use long division. $694,562 ÷ 22 = $31,571
6	D	Let the number of tickets to be sold be n. Therefore, n * 20 = 20000 n = 20000 / 20 n = 1000
7	D	Number of packages(n) = Total number of clips required/Number of clips in one package n = 3200 / 200 n = 16
8	D	Number of closets that can be built(n) = Total number of shelves/ Number of shelves in each closet n = 2592 / 108 n = 24
9	D	Use long division. $17,235 ÷ $45 = 383
10	B	Use the standard long division algorithm. 4,224 ÷ 12 = 352
11	1575	40950 / x = 26 x = 40950 / 26 x = 1575
12	65	We have to find the number, which when multiplied with 7 gives 455. Number x 7 = 455. Or Number = 455 divided by 7. Use the standard long division algorithm to get the answer: 65

Question No.	Answer	Detailed Explanation
		## Lesson 3: Operations With Decimals
1	A	$7.25 + $8.16 + $5.44 = $20.85 $20.85/3 = $6.95
2	D	The standard form would be written as 20.063 since the whole number part is 20 and the decimal part is written .063 (Sixty-three thousandths).
3	B	$160 + $12.50 = $172.50 (His total investment) $215.00 − $172.50 = $42.50
4	B	$11.50*20 = $230 $4.75*20 = $95 $230 − $95 = $135 $135.00 would be saved by purchasing the paperback book
5	D	The last set is the only set of numbers that are all equivalent. These numbers all have a decimal equivalent of 0.36.
6	C	1.29 + 0.85 + 3.63= 5.77 7.84 − 5.77 = 2.07 acres left to mow
7	B	Multiply the length by width to find the area. 5.8 * 17.2 Multiply the numbers and find the product. Then, count the decimal places in the factors. There is one decimal place for each factor or a total of two decimal places. Count two spaces from the right and put the decimal point in your answer. 5.8 * 17.2 = 99.76
8	A	The bushel of apples weighs 28.2 pounds. There are three people to split the apples. Solve by dividing the total weight of the apples by three. 28.2/3 = 9.4 pounds each
9	C	To figure out how far Joann and John hiked on Friday divide 67.8 by 2. 67.8 ÷ 2 = 33.9. Subtract 20 from 33.9 to find out how much farther they have to travel. 33.9 − 20 =13.9 miles
10	D	To find how much money each person earns per week, divide the total earned by 3. $72.00 ÷ 3 = $24.00 Then, to find how much one person makes over a four-week period, multiply by 4. $24.00 * 4= $96.00

Question No.	Answer	Detailed Explanation
11		A. 62.37 x 30 =1871.1 B. 6.237 x 30 =187.11 C. 0.6237 x 30 = 18.711 Because 6237 x 30 = 187,110 Problem A has 2 decimal places in the factors, so the product would have 2 decimal places: 1871.10 or 1871.1 Problem B has 3 decimal places in the factors, so the product would have 3 decimal places: 187.110 or 187.11 Problem C has 4 decimal places in the factors, so the product would have 4 decimal places: 18.7110 or 18.711
12	22.72	Answer is 22.72 Because 71 x 32 = 2272. The factors have a total of 2 decimal places, therefore the answer should have 2 decimal places: 22.72
13		When subtracting decimals, line up the decimal places horizontally. A. 9.13 -2.46 = 6.67 B. 913.00 - 2.46 = 910.54 C. 91.30 - 2.46 = 88.84

Question No.	Answer	Detailed Explanation
	## Lesson 4: Using Common Factors
1	D	All statements are true. A number is always a factor and a multiple of itself. It is prime because the only two factors are 1 and 17.
2	A	Other than 1, which is not prime by definition, 2, 3, 5, and 7 are the only single-digit numbers that can be divided by only themselves and 1.
3	C	A prime number is a whole number (greater than 1) which is divisible by only 1 and itself. The set {7, 23, 47} contains three numbers which fit the definition stated above. Each number is divisible by only 1 and itself.
4	D	(7*5) * x = 105 35x = 105 x = 3
5	C	The prime factorization of a number are the prime numbers that when multiplied together, give a product of the starting number. 240 = 120 x 2 120 = 60 x 2 60 = 30 x 2 30 = 15 x 2 15 = 5 x 3 2 x 2 x 2 x 2 x 3 x 5 = 240
6	C	Find the least multiple common to both numbers, starting with the greater number: 11: 11, 22, 33, 44, 55, 66, 77, 88... 5: 5, 10, 15, 20, 25, 30, 35, 40, 45, 50, 55 Stop when you get to the lowest multiple that is common to both. 55 is the LCM (lowest common multiple) of these two numbers, so each building could have 55 rooms.
7	C	When the sum of the digits in the number equals three or a multiple of 3, the number is divisible by 3. For example, 375 is divisible by 3 because 3 + 7 + 5 = 15 Because 15 is a multiple of 3, the number is divisible by 3.

Question No.	Answer	Detailed Explanation
8	B	42: 1, 2, 3, 6, 7, 14, 21, 42 56: 1, 2, 4, 7, 8, 14, 28, 56 The greatest common factor is 14.
9	D	Prime factorization is when a number is factored as far as possible into its prime factors. Start by factoring a number into two factors: 110 can be factored into two factors of 11 X 10. 11 is a prime number, so that is the first prime factor. 10 is composite so it can be factored into factors of 2 and 5. 2 and 5 are both prime numbers, so those are the remaining prime factors. Thus, the prime factorization of 110 is 2 X 5 X 11
10	D	To find the LCM, list the first few multiples of each number: 16: 16, 32, 48, 64 24: 24, 48, 72 48 is the least multiple that is common to both lists.
11	12	The Common Factors of 24, 36 and 48 are: 24: 1, 2, 3, 4, 6, 8, **12**, 24 36: 1, 2, 3, 4, 6, 9, **12**, 18, 36 48: 1, 2, 3, 4, 6, 8, **12**, 16, 24, 48 Hence, the Greatest Common Factor (GCF) is **12**.
12		1, 2, 4, 5, 10, 20 These are the numbers evenly divisible into the number 20.
13	A	Factors of 10: 1, 2, 5, 10 are the numbers evenly divisible into 10 Factors of 15: 1, 3, 5, 15 are the numbers evenly divisible into 15 So the common factors are 1 and 5.
14	1, 2, 4	Factors of 8: 1, 2, 4, 8 are the numbers evenly divisible into 8 Factors of 12: 1, 2, 3, 4, 6, 12 are the numbers evenly divisible into 12 So the common factors are 1, 2, and 4.

Question No.	Answer	Detailed Explanation

Lesson 5: Positive and Negative Numbers

Question No.	Answer	Detailed Explanation
1	D	Larissa has $4\frac{1}{2}$ cups of flour. Amount of flour needed to make cookies $= 2\frac{3}{4}$ cups of flour. Amount of flour left after making cookies $= 4\frac{1}{2}$ - $2\frac{3}{4}$ $4\frac{1}{2}$ - $2\frac{3}{4}$ $= \frac{9}{2}$ - $\frac{11}{4}$ $= \frac{9 \times 2}{2 \times 2}$ - $\frac{11}{4}$ $= \frac{18}{4}$ - $\frac{11}{4}$ $= \frac{18 - 11}{4}$ $= \frac{7}{4}$ $= 1\frac{3}{4}$
2	D	$\$2,123 - 2,400 = -\$277$ They must make a deposit of $277 in order to prevent the account from being overdrawn.
3	B	$1 + 4 - 2 = 3$
4	C	$\$26,247 + \$14,256 = \$40,503$ The net profit and the expenses must be added together to get the gross revenue.
5	A	Total snow at 6 p.m. = snow at 4 p.m. + snow fell between 4 p.m. to 6 p.m. = 6 + 4 = 10 inches
6	B	The change in temperature can be expressed as $5*(-2)$, or -10 degrees $20 + (-10) = 10$ degree F.
7	A	Call the basement 0, since the ground level would be considered the 1st floor. Tom's motion on the elevator can be described as $0 - 3 + 4 = 1$. He ends up on the 1st floor (ground level).
8	A	$\frac{43}{6}$ simplifies to 7 and $\frac{1}{6}$, which is larger than 7. All other fractions are greater than 6 but less than 7.
9	C	$652 - 491 = 161$ feet Because Stacey started out above sea level and does not go below zero, you know the town is 161 feet above sea level.
10	B	$-53 + 27 = -26$
11	A, C, & D	In choice A and C, the negative numbers are larger than the positive number. In choice D, two negatives subtracted will result in a negative answer.
12	57	Answer is 57, because from 0 to 30 is a difference of 30 steps; 0 to -27 is a difference of 27 steps. Combined, this is a difference of 57 steps on the number line.
13	-15	Because -15 is the number that would lie farthest left on a number line. Numbers increase in value as they move to the right on a number line.

Question No.	Answer	Detailed Explanation

Lesson 6: Representing Negative Numbers

Question No.	Answer	Detailed Explanation
1	D	−4 is only 4 units away from 0 on a number line. All of the other numbers are farther away.
2	A	If you count the units between −5.5 and 7.5, you will count 13 units between them.
3	D	 The number line above shows −1, 3, and 4. All other answer choices are not represented on this number line.
4	A	Moving left on the number line indicates moving in a negative direction. Moving right on the number line indicates moving in a positive direction.
5	A	−7.2 is less than −7 so it would not be found between −7 and −4.
6	D	−7.25 is less than −7 but greater than −8 so it would be the number found between −7 and −8.
7	C	Additive inverse of a given number has the same magnitude with opposite sign. $4 + (−4) = 0$
8	B	{1, −4, −5} is the only set which would fall to the left of 4 on a number line. Any number larger than 4 would fall to the right on a number line and would not fit the criteria.
9	D	$+12 + (−21) + 3 = −6$
10	C	The only number that would fall between 0 and −1 would be −0.8, as $−1 < −0.8 < 0$
11	A	Answer is -17. Because it is only 17 numbers away from 0 whereas the other the other two options are 28 and 36 numbers away from 0. (Closest to 0 when dealing with negative numbers has the highest value).
12	A, C, & D	3 is a positive number, therefore it is greater than 0. All negative numbers are less than 0.

Question No.	Answer	Detailed Explanation
		Lesson 7: Ordered Pairs
1	B	Quadrant II – In this quadrant the x-coordinate is negative and the y-coordinate is positive.
2	D	Quadrant IV – In this quadrant the x-coordinate is positive and the y-coordinate is negative.
3	C	Quadrant III – In this quadrant both the x-coordinate and y-coordinate are negative.
4	C	When a point is reflected across the x-axis the x-coordinate remains the same and the y-coordinate changes sign. (10, −4) → (10, 4)
5	D	When a point is reflected across the y-axis the y-coordinate remains the same and the x-coordinate changes sign. (6, 3) → (−6, 3)
6	A	When a point is reflected across the x-axis the x-coordinate remains the same and the y-coordinate changes sign. C (2, 9) → C′ (2, −9). When a point is reflected across the y-axis the y-coordinate remains the same and the x-coordinate changes sign. C′ (2, −9) → C″ (−2, −9)
7	D	Quadrant I: (3,4); (6,14) 2 Quadrant II: (−2,4) 1 Quadrant III: (−9,−5), (−5,−11); (−99, −43) 3 Quadrant IV: (3,−2); (4,−3), (1,−3); (4,−12) 4 Quadrant IV has the most points.
8	C	In Quadrant II the x-coordinate is negative and the y-coordinate is positive. When a point is reflect across the y-axis the y-coordinate remains the same and the x-coordinate changes sign. Therefore points with a positive x-coordinate and a positive y-coordinate will fall in Quadrant II when reflected across the y-axis. Therefore two of the points will fall in Quadrant II when reflected across the y-axis: (5,1) and (7,12).
9	A	Reflection of A(4,0) is A′(-4,0). It should have been graphed four units to the left of the origin. (Note: when the point (0,0) is reflected across the y-axis it remains in the same position.)
10	A	When a point is reflected across the x-axis the x-coordinate remains the same and the y-coordinate changes sign. (12, −4) → (12, 4) The point (12,4) is located in Quadrant I.
11	C	(-3,2) because the point is in the Quadrant II, where x - coordinate is negative and y - coordinate is positive. The given point is 2 units above x-axis so y coordinate = 2 and the point is 3 units to the left of y-axis so x coordinate = -3
12	(6,4)	(6,4) because the plotted point is 6 lines on the horizontally x-axis and four lines vertically on the y-axis.

Lesson 8: Number Line & Coordinate Plane

Question No.	Answer	Detailed Explanation
1	C	Distance between 9 and 16 = 7. Distance between two consecutive ticks = 7/7 = 1. Therefore the dot represents the number 14.
2	C	Distance between -5 and 3 = 8. Distance between two consecutive ticks = 8/8 = 1. Therefore the dot represents the number 0.
3	C	Distance between -2 and 14 = 16. Distance between two consecutive ticks = 16/8 = 2. Therefore the dot represents the number 4.
4	B	Distance between -10 and -6 = 4. Distance between two consecutive ticks = 4/8 = 0.5. Therefore the dot represents the number -7.5.
5	C	Distance between -25 and +25 = 50. Distance between two consecutive ticks = 50/10 = 5. Therefore the dot represents the number 5.
6	B	An ordered pair is written in the format (x,y) where x is the first number and y is the second number. The point $(1, -2)$ is located 1 unit to the right (x-axis) and 2 units down (y-axis) from the origin. This is represented by Point B.
7	A	An ordered pair is written in the format (x,y) where x is the first number and y is the second number. The point $(-3, 5)$ is located 3 units to the left (x-axis) and 5 units up (y-axis) from the origin. This is represented by Point A.
8	B	An ordered pair is written in the format (x,y) where x is the first number and y is the second number. The point $(-4, -5)$ is located 4 units to the left (x-axis) and 5 units down (y-axis) from the origin. This is represented by Point B.
9	B	An ordered pair is written in the format (x,y) where x is the first number and y is the second number. The point $(-1.5, 0.5)$ is located 1.5 units to the left (x-axis) and 0.5 units up (y-axis) from the origin. This is represented by Point B.
10	C	(3,4) = Point A (−2,4) = Point B (3,2) is not plotted (−4, −3) = Point D
11	F	To find the point which is represented by the ordered pair (-9, -2), move 9 units from the origin to the left and 2 units down. From the graph we see that this represents point F.
12	B & C	Negative numbers are smaller than zero. Positive numbers are greater than zero. (B) and(C) are correct.

Lesson 9: Absolute Value

Question No.	Answer	Detailed Explanation
1	B	$17 - |(7)(-3)|$ $= 17 - |-21|$ $= 17 - 21$ $= -4$ Note: Absolute value (the value of $|x|$) is the value of a number without regard to its sign.
2	A	$16 + |(7)(-3) - 44| - 5$ $= 16 + |-21 - 44| - 5$ $= 16 + |-21 + (-44)| - 5$ $= 16 + |-65| - 5$ $= 16 + 65 - 5$ $= 81 - 5$ $= 76$ Note: Absolute value (the value of $|x|$) is the value of a number without regard to its sign.
3	A	$|15 - 47| + 9 - |(-2)(-4) - 17|$ $= |-32| + 9 - |8 - 17|$ $= 32 + 9 - |-9|$ $= 32 + 9 - 9$ $= 41-9$ $= 32$ Note: Absolute value (the value of $|x|$) is the value of a number without regard to its sign.
4	A	$18 + 3|6 - 25| - 11$ $= 18 + 3|-19| - 11$ $= 18 + 3(19) - 11$ $= 18 + 57 - 11$ $= 18 + 57 - 11$ $= 75 - 11$ $= 64$ Note: Absolute value (the value of $|x|$) is the value of a number without regard to its sign.
5	A	$77 - |(-8)(3) + (-10)(4)|$ $= 77 - |(-24) + (-40)|$ $= 77 - |-64|$ $= 77 - 64$ $= 13$ Note: Absolute value (the value of $|x|$) is the value of a number without regard to its sign.

Question No.	Answer	Detailed Explanation
6	D	$21 - \lvert 8 -(-5)(7) \rvert - 54$ $= 21 - \lvert 8 - (-35) \rvert - 54$ $= 21 - \lvert 8 + 35 \rvert - 54$ $= 21 - \lvert 43 \rvert - 54$ $= 21 - (43) - 54$ $= 21 + (-43) - 54$ $= -22 - 54$ $= -22 + (-54)$ $= -76$ Note: Absolute value (the value of $\lvert x \rvert$) is the value of a number without regard to its sign.
7	C	Two values could satisfy the equation. For k = 2, $\lvert 9 - 3*2 \rvert = \lvert 9 - 6 \rvert = 3$ For k = 4, $\lvert 9 - 3*4 \rvert = \lvert 9 - 12 \rvert = \lvert -3 \rvert = 3$
8	A	The absolute value of a non-zero number is always positive.
9	C	The absolute value of a number is always positive. In this case, however, there is a negative sign outside the absolute value bars, which stands for -1, which is to be multiplied by $\lvert 24 \rvert$. Thus, $-1*24 = -24$
10	C	$\lvert 45 - 75 \rvert$ $= \lvert -30 \rvert$ $= 30$
11	- 14	$\lvert 14 \rvert - \lvert -28 \rvert$ $= 14 - 28 = -14$
12	$\lvert -25 \rvert$	$\lvert -25 \rvert$ because the absolute value of -25 is 25 which is higher than 24.

Question No.	Answer	Detailed Explanation

Lesson 10: Rational Numbers in Context

1	A	-7 is greater than -12 so Xavier has the higher score.
2	A	Get a common denominator and compare fractions. The LCM between 6 and 12 is 12. Kelly: $\frac{(5 \times 2)}{(6 \times 2)} = \frac{10}{12}$ Helen: $\frac{9}{12}$ Kelly has read more because $\frac{10}{12} > \frac{9}{12}$ or $\frac{5}{6} > \frac{9}{12}$.
3	D	$-52°F > -80°F$ $-52°F$ is 52 degrees below zero whereas $-80°F$ is 80 degrees below zero.
4	B	Rewrite these three numbers all as decimals or fractions. $1\frac{3}{4} = 1.75$ $\frac{20}{8} = 2.5$ $1.6 = 1.6$ Now compare: $2.5 > 1.75 > 1.6$ Now rewrite them in their original form: $\frac{20}{8} > 1\frac{3}{4} > 1.6$
5	D	-143 means 143 feet below sea level. -134 feet means 134 feet below sea level. Therefore Doug dove deeper because he went further below sea level than Sissy.
6	C	Rewrite these three numbers all as decimals or fractions. $\frac{4}{15} = 0.27$ $0.4 = 0.4$ $\frac{1}{3} = 0.33$ Now compare: $0.4 > 0.33 > 0.27$ Now rewrite them in their original form: $0.4 > \frac{1}{3} > \frac{4}{15}$
7	C	15 feet below sea level $= -15$ feet $\frac{33}{3} = 11$ feet below sea level $= -11$ feet 11.5 feet below sea level $= -11.5$ feet The deepest school is the one with the greater negative magnitude. Therefore: -15 is deeper than -11.5 is deeper than -11 or $S1 > S3 > S2$.

Question No.	Answer	Detailed Explanation
8	A	Get a common denominator and compare fractions. The LCM between 5 and 7 is 35. $\frac{(4 \times 7)}{(5 \times 7)} = \frac{28}{35}$ $\frac{(5 \times 5)}{(7 \times 5)} = \frac{25}{35}$ It snowed more on the first day because $\frac{28}{35} > \frac{25}{35}$ or $\frac{4}{5} > \frac{5}{7}$.
9	B	First determine the balance of Molly's account: $365 - $415 = -$50$ Molly has a balance of $-$50$ so she owes the bank $50. Bill has a balance of $-$45$ so he owes the bank $45. Therefore Molly owes the bank more than Bill.
10	B	Jeremiah has eaten $2\frac{5}{6}$ boxes. Farley has eaten $1\frac{15}{9} = 2\frac{6}{9}$ Since they both have eaten 2 boxes lets determine which is greater $\frac{5}{6}$ or $\frac{6}{9}$ The LCM of 6 and 9 is 18. $\frac{(5 \times 3)}{(6 \times 3)} = \frac{15}{18}$, $\frac{(6 \times 2)}{(9 \times 2)} = \frac{12}{18}$ Since $\frac{15}{18} > \frac{12}{18}$ Jeremiah has eaten more, therefore Farley has more left.
11	56	The answer is 56 degrees. Comparing the 2 values, 32 or 56, 56 degrees would be hotter when compared to 32 degrees.
12	B & C	-3 and 25 are the correct answers. On a number line, -3 and 25 are the only numbers which would fall to the right of -5, which means they are greater than -5.

Question No.	Answer	Detailed Explanation
	**Lesson 11: Interpreting Absolute Value**

Question No.	Answer	Detailed Explanation
1	C	The absolute value of a number is its distance from zero on a number line. Distance between two consecutive ticks on the number line is 1 unit. So the number represented by the dot is 3. The $\mid 3 \mid$ is 3 because it is three units from 0.
2	C	The absolute value of a number is its distance from zero on a number line. Distance between two consecutive ticks on the number line is 0.5 units. So the number represented by the dot is -1. The $\mid -1 \mid$ is 1 because it is 1 unit from 0.
3	A	The absolute value of a number is its distance from zero on a number line. $\mid -27 \mid = 27$ and $27 > 19$. Therefore $\mid -27 \mid > 19$.
4	A	The absolute value of a number is its distance from zero on a number line. $- \mid -6 \mid$ or the negative of the absolute value of -6 is -6 and $-4 > -6$. Therefore $-4 > - \mid -6 \mid$.
5	B	To make the statement $-12 < x$ true, x must be greater than -12. To make the statement $\mid x \mid < 4$, x must be greater than -4 and less than 4. The only answer choice meeting these criteria is $x = -1$.
6	D	$\mid 30 \mid = 30$ $\mid 24 \mid = 24$ $\mid -30 \mid = 30$ Therefore both 30 and -30 have the greater absolute value.
7	D	$\mid 215 \mid = \$215$ $\mid -100 \mid = \$100$ $\mid -250 \mid = \$250$ $100 < 215 < 250$ or $\mid -100 \mid < \mid 215 \mid < \mid -250 \mid$
8	C	**True**. Betsy is 6.2 meters away from the center buoy and Luis is 6.5 meters away. Betsy is closer by 0.3 meters. **True**. Luis is 6.5 meters from the center buoy. **False**. Betsy is 6.2 meters away from the center buoy and Luis is 6.5 meters away. Luis is 0.3 meters farther from the buoy. **True**. Betsy is 6.2 meters directly south of the center buoy which is 6.5 meters directly south of Luis therefore Betsy is $6.2 + 6.5 = 12.7$ meters from Luis.

Question No.	Answer	Detailed Explanation
9	D	Ophelia: $157 - 145 = 12$ pounds; $\lvert 12 \rvert = 12$ Aaron: $163 - 178 = -15$ pounds: $\lvert -15 \rvert = 15$ Nathan: $217 - 205 = 12$ pounds; $\lvert 12 \rvert = 12$ Rebecca: $128 - 136 = -8$ pounds; $\lvert -8 \rvert = 8$ Rebecca has the least absolute change of 8 pounds.
10	A	New York: $108 - (-52) = 160$ Texas: $120 - (-23) = 143$ Florida: $109 - (-2) = 111$ North Carolina: $110 - (-34) = 144$ New York has experienced the broadest range of temperature extremes.
11		-5, -1, 2 because negative numbers fall to the left of the 0.
12	E	-10 has the highest absolute value because it is 10 points away from 0.

Question No.	Answer	Detailed Explanation
		Lesson 12: Comparisons of Absolute Value
1	B	A negative account balance indicates a debt is owed. −$45 means $45 is owed. −$5 means $5 is owed. Therefore the account balance of −$45 represents the greatest debt.
2	A	The warmer temperatures are above zero. Of these two 5°F > 2°F . Therefore the warmest temperature is 5°F above zero.
3	A	First calculate the amount Anneliese spent: $58.00 + $35.00 = $93.00. If her account balance is −$142.00 then before she spent any money she had −$142.00 + $93.00 = −$49.00.
4	B	First calculate the elevation of the campground. They climbed to an elevation of 1839 feet and then descended 527 feet to the restaurant. So the restaurant is located at 1839 − 527 = 1312 feet. The campground is 264 feet higher than the restaurant and so is located at 1312 + 264 = 1576 feet. The difference in elevation between home and the campground is 1576 − 439 = 1137 feet.
5	C	Find the total debits and credits. Debits: (2*$5.99) + $28.00 = $39.98 Credits: $46.50 Now determine the account balance: $165.00 − $39.98 + $46.50 = $171.52
6	C	Dominik: 28 feet Denzel: −5.3 feet (5.3 feet below sea level) Kaila: −7 feet (7 feet below sea level) Malik: 20 feet The lowest elevation is −7 feet where Kaila lives.
7	D	14.9 below zero = −14.9 5.1 below zero = −5.1 6 above zero = 6 15 above zero = 15 The warmest temperature is the greatest positive number or 15 degrees C in Death Valley, California.
8	D	Sato: +4 inches Ichiro: −2 inches Aran: +6 inches Mio: −2.5 inches The shortest person is Mio.

Question No.	Answer	Detailed Explanation
9	C	Find how much Leary spent by subtracting the change he received from the amount of money he started with. $60.00 − $3.72 = $56.28
10	B	Find the total debits and credits. Debits: $75.38 + $35.00 = $110.38 Credits: $26.16 Now determine the account balance: $629.00 − $110.38 + $26.16 =$544.78
11	A, B, C, & D	All of the answers have a distance of less than 20 from zero, which means they have an absolute value less than 20.
12	1	Answer is 1, because the absolute value of 12 is 12, and that of -11 is 11. So 12 - 11 = 1.

Question No.	Answer	Detailed Explanation

Lesson 13: Coordinate Plane

Question No.	Answer	Detailed Explanation
1	B	Move on the x axis from −3.6, four units to the right to 0.4 (East is to the right on this map.) Then move on the y axis from −2.6, six units up to 3.4 (North is up on this map.) So, the coordinates are (0.4, 3.4).
2	D	In Quadrant II, the x value is negative and the y value is positive. The coordinates would be (−5, 8).
3	B	Absolute value is the positive value of a number. That makes the ordered pair (4, 4).
4	A	Greg starts at (0,0). He moves north (up) 5 units and west (left) 3 units. That puts him at (−3, 5).
5	C	Point C is at (−4, 5) and Point D is at (−5, −2). That means that Yolanda has to walk 1 unit west (left) and 7 units south (down).
6	D	The coordinates of Point D are (−5, −2). Absolute value is the positive value of a number. That means the absolute value is (5, 2).
7	C	The x coordinate is listed first in a coordinate pair, and the y coordinate is listed second. The absolute value of a number is its positive value. In Quadrant IV, the x coordinate is positive and the y coordinate is negative. That makes the coordinates (7, −3).
8	D	The x coordinate is listed first in a coordinate pair, and the y coordinate is listed second. The absolute value of a number is its positive value. In Quadrant II, the x coordinate is negative and the y coordinate is positive. That makes the coordinates (−3,9).
9	C	The point (0, −6) is located 6 units below the x axis. If y = 0 is sea level, the point (0, −6) is 6 units below sea level.
10	D	The x coordinate is negative and the y coordinate is positive in Quadrant II. In Quadrant IV, the x coordinate is positive, and the y coordinate is negative making the coordinates (2,−8).
11	5	The coordinates of the point in the 1st quadrant are - (3,4) and that of the point in 2nd quadrant are (-2,4). So the distance between these points will be 3-(-2) = 5

Question No.	Answer	Detailed Explanation
12	B, D & E	Coordinates mentioned in options (B), (D) and (E) would fall in Quadrant I (Q I) because, points in Q I have positive x - coordinates and positive y - coordinates.
13	Point E	Given ordered pair is (0, -8). Its x - coordinate is zero. It means, the point is on the Y axis. Y - coordinate of the ordered pair is -8. It means, the point is below the origin and 8 units away from the origin. It is clear from the graph that Point E satisfies these conditions.

Chapter 4:
Expressions & Equations

Lesson 1: Whole Number Exponents

You can scan the QR code given below or use the url to access additional EdSearch resources including videos and mobile apps related to *Whole Number Exponents*.

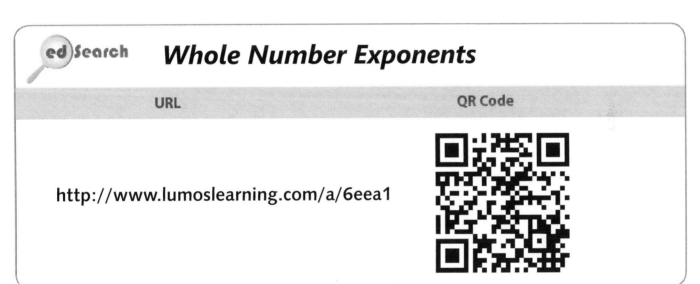

ed Search

Whole Number Exponents

URL	QR Code
http://www.lumoslearning.com/a/6eea1	

1. **Evaluate:** 5^3

    (A) 15
    (B) 125
    (C) 8
    (D) 2

2. **Write the expression using an exponent:** 2 * 2 * 2 * 2 * 2 * 2

    (A) 2 * 6
    (B) 12
    (C) 2^6
    (D) 6^2

3. **Write the expression using an exponent:** y * y * y * y

    (A) 4y
    (B) y/4
    (C) 4^y
    (D) y^4

4. **Find the numerical value of the following expression:** 11^1

    (A) 11
    (B) 1
    (C) 12
    (D) 10

5. **Write an expression using exponents:** 2 * 2 * m * m

    (A) 2(2m)
    (B) 4m
    (C) 2^2m^2
    (D) 2/m

6. **Simplify:** $4^3 * 4^2$

    (A) 20
    (B) 9
    (C) 4^5
    (D) 20

7. **Simplify: $(b^2c)(bc^3)$**

   (A) 3b/4
   (B) 3b * 4
   (C) b^3c^4
   (D) bc

8. **Simplify: $(n^4x^2)^3$**

   (A) 12n*6x
   (B) $n^{12}x^6$
   (C) $n^{43}x^{23}$
   (D) n^7x^5

9. **Simplify: $7^4/7^2$**

   (A) 7^6
   (B) 7^3
   (C) 7^2
   (D) 7^4

10. **Simplify: $[(3^5)(3^2)]^4$**

    (A) 3^{28}
    (B) 3^{40}
    (C) 3^{10}
    (D) 3^{11}

11. **Select all numbers that would have a total value greater than 50.**

    (A) 6^2
    (B) 2^3
    (C) 5^2
    (D) 10^2
    (E) 4^4

12. **Find the numerical value of 8^4. Write your answer in standard form in the box.**

Chapter 4

Lesson 2: Expressions Involving Variables

You can scan the QR code given below or use the url to access additional EdSearch resources including videos and mobile apps related to *Expressions Involving Variables*.

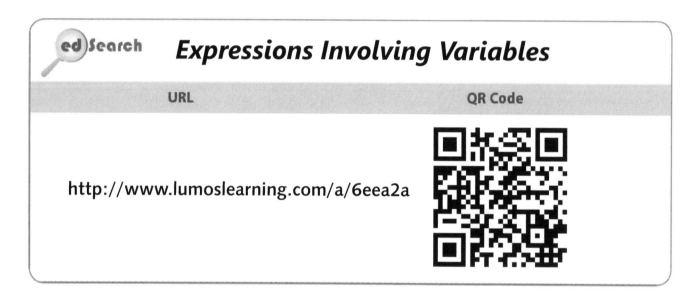

ed Search **Expressions Involving Variables**

URL	QR Code
http://www.lumoslearning.com/a/6eea2a	

LumosLearning.com

1. When the expression 3(n + 7) is evaluated for a given value of n, the result is 33. What is the value of n?

Ⓐ n = 4
Ⓑ n = 5
Ⓒ n = 21
Ⓓ n = 120

2. Which number is acting as a coefficient in this expression? 360 + 22x – 448

Ⓐ 360
Ⓑ 22
Ⓒ 448
Ⓓ None of these

3. Evaluate the following when n = 7: 5(n – 5)

Ⓐ 10
Ⓑ –60
Ⓒ 60
Ⓓ 30

4. For which of the following values of b does the expression 4b – 9 have a value between 90 and 100?

Ⓐ b = 104
Ⓑ b = 26
Ⓒ b = 48
Ⓓ b = 24

5. Evaluate the following when n = –4: [5n – 3n] + 2n

Ⓐ b = 16
Ⓑ b = –20
Ⓒ b = –16
Ⓓ b = 0

6. Translate the following: "Four times a number n is equal to the difference between that number and 10"

Ⓐ 4n = 10 – n
Ⓑ 4 + n = 10*n
Ⓒ 4/n = n + 10
Ⓓ 4n = n – 10

7. **Evaluate 2y + 3y − y when y = 2.**

   Ⓐ 7
   Ⓑ 8
   Ⓒ 9
   Ⓓ 10

8. **Find the value of 2b − 4 + 6y when b = 2 and y = 3.**

   Ⓐ 16
   Ⓑ 18
   Ⓒ 0
   Ⓓ −12

9. **Translate the following, and then solve: "A number n times 16 is equal to 48."**

   Ⓐ 16n = 48, n = 4
   Ⓑ 16n = 48, n = 8
   Ⓒ 16 + n = 48, n = 32
   Ⓓ 16n = 48, n = 3

10. **For which value of x does 6x + 12 evaluate to 54?**

    Ⓐ x = 12
    Ⓑ x = 9
    Ⓒ x = 7
    Ⓓ x = 6

11. **Circle the answer choice that represents "12 less than f".**

    Ⓐ 12 - f
    Ⓑ (12)f
    Ⓒ f - 12

12. **Which of the following represents the phrase "the quotient of 17 and q"? Select all the correct answers.**

    Ⓐ q ÷ 17
    Ⓑ 17 ÷ q
    Ⓒ 17/q
    Ⓓ q/17

Chapter 4

Lesson 3: Identifying Expression Parts

You can scan the QR code given below or use the url to access additional EdSearch resources including videos and mobile apps related to *Identifying Expression Parts*.

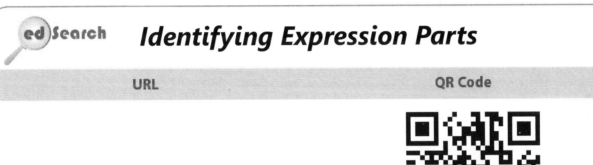

ed Search   *Identifying Expression Parts*

URL	QR Code
http://www.lumoslearning.com/a/6eea2b	

1. **Which of the following describes the expression 6(4−2) accurately?**

   Ⓐ Six and the difference of four and two.
   Ⓑ The product of six and the sum of four and two.
   Ⓒ The product of six and the difference of 4 and 2.
   Ⓓ The quotient of six and the difference of four and two.

2. **Which of the following describes the expression (8÷2)−10 accurately?**

   Ⓐ The quotient of eight and two subtracted from ten.
   Ⓑ Ten less than the quotient of eight and two.
   Ⓒ The difference of ten and the quotient of eight and two.
   Ⓓ The product of eight and two minus ten.

3. **What are the coefficients in the expression $(2x + 15)(9x - 3)$?**

   Ⓐ 2, 15, 9, −3
   Ⓑ 15, 3
   Ⓒ 15, −3
   Ⓓ 2, 9

4. **What is the value of the greatest coefficient in the expression $4a^2 + 9a - 11b^2 + 15$?**

   Ⓐ 4
   Ⓑ 9
   Ⓒ 11
   Ⓓ 15

5. **How many factors are in the following expression, 4(6 + 8) × 3(2 − 5)?**

   Ⓐ 2
   Ⓑ 4
   Ⓒ 5
   Ⓓ 6

6. **Which of the following describes the expression $4÷(5 \times \dfrac{1}{2})$ accurately?**

   Ⓐ The quotient of 4 and $5\dfrac{1}{2}$

   Ⓑ divided by the quotient of 5 and $\dfrac{1}{2}$

   Ⓒ The quotient of 4 and the product of 5 and $\dfrac{1}{2}$

   Ⓓ The product of 5 and $\dfrac{1}{2}$ divided by 4.

7. Which of the following describes the expression (6+9) – 4 accurately?

Ⓐ 4 subtracted from the sum of 6 and 9.
Ⓑ The sum of 6 and 9 subtracted from 4.
Ⓒ The difference of 6 and 9 less 4.
Ⓓ The sum of the quantity of 6 plus 9 and 4.

8. Which term has the smallest coefficient in the expression $8x^4 + \frac{7}{8}x^3 - 2x^2 + x$?

Ⓐ 1st term
Ⓑ 2nd term
Ⓒ 3rd term
Ⓓ 4th term

9. Which of the following accurately represents "The product of 15 and the sum of 9 and 7."?

Ⓐ 15 + (9 × 7)
Ⓑ (15 + 9) × 7
Ⓒ 15 ÷ (9 + 7)
Ⓓ 15(9 + 7)

10. Which of the following describes the expression (12 ÷ 4) + [2 × (−2)] accurately?

Ⓐ The sum of the quotient of 12 and 4 and the product of 2 and −2.
Ⓑ The quotient of 12 and 4 plus the difference of the product of 2 and 2.
Ⓒ The quotient of 4 and 12 plus the product of 2 and −2.
Ⓓ The difference of 2 times −2 and the quotient of 12 and 4.

11. Which of the following means the same as 3(2+1)? Select all the correct answers.

Ⓐ (2+1) + (2+1) + (2+1)
Ⓑ 6 + 3
Ⓒ 3 + 2 +1
Ⓓ (6 + 1) + (6 + 1) + (6 + 1)
Ⓔ None of the above

12. _____ is the same as (3+1) + (3+1). Circle the correct answer choice.

Ⓐ 2(3+1)
Ⓑ 3(2+1)
Ⓒ (3+1)^2

Chapter 4

Lesson 4: Evaluating Expressions

You can scan the QR code given below or use the url to access additional EdSearch resources including videos and mobile apps related to *Evaluating Expressions*.

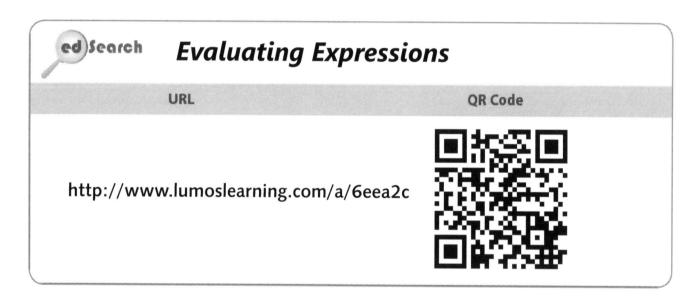

ed)Search *Evaluating Expressions*

URL	QR Code
http://www.lumoslearning.com/a/6eea2c	

1. **What is the value of y in the equation $y = 3x - 13$, when x = 6?**

   Ⓐ 5
   Ⓑ −4
   Ⓒ −1
   Ⓓ 4

2. **What is the value of y in the equation $y = \dfrac{1}{4} x \div 2$, when x = 32?**

   Ⓐ 2
   Ⓑ 4
   Ⓒ 8
   Ⓓ 10

3. **Evaluate the following expression when a = 3 and b = −8: $3a^2 - 7b$**

   Ⓐ −44
   Ⓑ −29
   Ⓒ 68
   Ⓓ 83

4. **Evaluate the following expression when v = −2 and w = 155: $6v^3 + \dfrac{4}{5} w$**

   Ⓐ 17
   Ⓑ 68
   Ⓒ 76
   Ⓓ 172

5. **Evaluate the following expression when c = −3 and d = 2: $\dfrac{6}{d} - 10c - c^4$**

   Ⓐ −108
   Ⓑ −48
   Ⓒ 39
   Ⓓ 114

6. **Use the formula $V = s^3$ to find the volume of a cube with a side length of 2 cm.**

   Ⓐ 4 cm²
   Ⓑ 6 cm³
   Ⓒ 8 cm³
   Ⓓ 9 cm³

7. Use the formula $A = l \times w$ to find the area of a rectangle with a length of 4.5 feet and a width of 7.3 feet.

Ⓐ 28.15 ft²
Ⓑ 30.35 ft²
Ⓒ 32.35 ft²
Ⓓ 32.85 ft²

8. Leah found a cylindrical container with a radius of $1\frac{1}{2}$ inches and a height of 11 inches. Use the formula $V = \pi r^2 h$, where $\pi = 3.14$, r is the radius and h is the height, to find the volume of the container. Round to the nearest hundredth.

Ⓐ 51.81 in³
Ⓑ 77.72 in³
Ⓒ 103.62 in³
Ⓓ 566.28 in³

9. What is the area of a square with a side of $\frac{3}{4}$ meter, $A = s^2$, where A is the area of the square, s it's length.

Ⓐ $\frac{3}{16}$ m²

Ⓑ $\frac{9}{16}$ m²

Ⓒ $\frac{3}{4}$ m²

Ⓓ $\frac{9}{4}$ m²

10. The area of the base of a square pyramid is 10 ft² and the height is 6 ft. What is the volume of the pyramid using the formula $V = \frac{1}{3}\beta h$, where β is the area of the base and h is the height?

Ⓐ 20 ft³
Ⓑ 60 ft³
Ⓒ 200 ft³
Ⓓ 600 ft³

11. Circle the answer that fits the 'x' in this equation $\dfrac{1200}{x} = 30$.

    Ⓐ 4

    Ⓑ 40

    Ⓒ 400

12. Select the equations in which j = 7. Choose all that apply.

    Ⓐ $3j - 4 = 25$

    Ⓑ $56 - j = 49$

    Ⓒ $3j + 4 = 25$

    Ⓓ $j^3 = 343$

Chapter 4

Lesson 5: Writing Equivalent Expressions

You can scan the QR code given below or use the url to access additional EdSearch resources including videos and mobile apps related to *Writing Equivalent Expressions*.

URL	QR Code
http://www.lumoslearning.com/a/6eea3	

1. **What is an equivalent expression for 3n − 12?**

   Ⓐ 3n + 1
   Ⓑ 3n + 4
   Ⓒ 3n − 4
   Ⓓ 3(n − 4)

2. **Simplify 2n − 7n to create an equivalent expression.**

   Ⓐ 5n
   Ⓑ −5n
   Ⓒ −n(2 − 7)
   Ⓓ n(5)

3. **Which expression is equivalent to 5y + 2z − 3y + z?**

   Ⓐ z
   Ⓑ 2y + 3z
   Ⓒ yz
   Ⓓ 11yz

4. **Which expression is equivalent to 8a + 9 − 3(a + 4)?**

   Ⓐ 32 − 3a
   Ⓑ a
   Ⓒ 24a
   Ⓓ 5a − 3

5. **Which inequality has the same solution set as 3(q + 6) > 11?**

   Ⓐ 3q + 18 < 11
   Ⓑ 3q + 18 > 11
   Ⓒ 3q + 6 > 11
   Ⓓ q + 18 > 11

6. **Which inequality has the same solution set as 10 < q + q + q + q + q − 5?**

   Ⓐ 10 > 5q + 5
   Ⓑ 10 < 5q + 5
   Ⓒ 10 > 5q − 5
   Ⓓ 10 < 5q − 5

7. **Simplify the following equation:**
   u + u + u + u − p + p + p − r = 55

   Ⓐ 4u + 2p − r = 55
   Ⓑ 4u + p − r = 55
   Ⓒ 4u − 3p + r = 55
   Ⓓ 4u − 3p − r = 55

8. **36x − 12 = 108 has the same solution(s) as** _____ .

   Ⓐ 3(3x − 12) = 108
   Ⓑ 12(3x −1) = 108
   Ⓒ 3(12x − 12) = 108
   Ⓓ 12(x−1) = 108

9. **Why is the expression 5(3x + 2) equivalent to 15x + 10?**

   Ⓐ The 5 has been divided into each term in parentheses.
   Ⓑ The 5 was distributed using the Distributive Property.
   Ⓒ The 5 was distributed using the Associative Property.
   Ⓓ The expressions are not equal.

10. **Which expression is equivalent to 5b − 9c − 2(4b + c)?**

    Ⓐ −3b + 7c
    Ⓑ −3b − 7c
    Ⓒ −3b −11c
    Ⓓ −3b + 11c

11. **Write the correct equation for the following expression. "3 less than the product of 4 and 5."**

12. **Circle the answer that represents 2(4+3b).**

    Ⓐ 8 + 6b
    Ⓑ 6 + 8b
    Ⓒ 6b - 8

Chapter 4

Lesson 6: Identifying Equivalent Expressions

You can scan the QR code given below or use the url to access additional EdSearch resources including videos and mobile apps related to *Identifying Equivalent Expressions*.

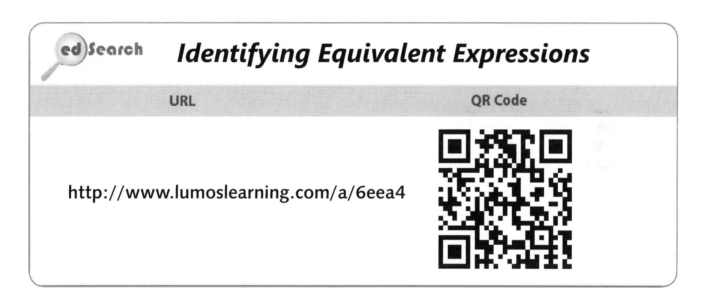

URL	QR Code
http://www.lumoslearning.com/a/6eea4	

1. **Which two expressions are equivalent?**

   Ⓐ $(\frac{5}{25})x$ and $(\frac{1}{3})x$

   Ⓑ $(\frac{5}{25})x$ and $(\frac{1}{5})x$

   Ⓒ $(\frac{5}{25})x$ and $(\frac{1}{4})x$

   Ⓓ $(\frac{5}{25})x$ and $(\frac{1}{6})x$

2. **Which two expressions are equivalent?**

   Ⓐ $7 + 21v$ and $2(5 + 3v)$
   Ⓑ $7 + 21v$ and $3(4 + 7v)$
   Ⓒ $7 + 21v$ and $7(1 + 3v)$
   Ⓓ $7 + 21v$ and $7(7 + 21v)$

3. **Which two expressions are equivalent?**

   Ⓐ $\frac{32p}{2}$ and $17p$

   Ⓑ $\frac{32p}{2}$ and $18p$

   Ⓒ $\frac{32p}{2}$ and $16p$

   Ⓓ $\frac{32p}{2}$ and $14p$

4. **Which two expressions are equivalent?**

   Ⓐ $17(3m + 4)$ and $51m + 68$
   Ⓑ $17(3m + 4)$ and $51m + 67$
   Ⓒ $17(3m + 4)$ and $51m - 68$
   Ⓓ $17(3m + 4)$ and $47m + 51$

5. **Which two expressions are equivalent?**

   Ⓐ $\frac{64k}{4}$ and $4k$

   Ⓑ $\frac{64k}{4}$ and $14k$

   Ⓒ $\frac{64k}{4}$ and $16k$

   Ⓓ $\frac{64k}{4}$ and $15k$

6. **575d – 100 is equivalent to:**

   Ⓐ 25(23d − 4)
   Ⓑ 25(22d − 4)
   Ⓒ 25(23d + 4)
   Ⓓ 25(25d − 4)

7. **(800 + 444y)/4 is equivalent to:**

   Ⓐ 200 + 44y
   Ⓑ 800 + 111y
   Ⓒ 200 + 111y
   Ⓓ 200 − 111y

8. **5(19 −8y) is equivalent to:**

   Ⓐ 95 − 35y
   Ⓑ 95 + 40y
   Ⓒ 85 − 40y
   Ⓓ 95 − 40y

9. **The expression 3(26p − 7 + 14h) is equivalent to:**

   Ⓐ 78 − 21 + 42
   Ⓑ 78p + 21 + 42h
   Ⓒ 78p − 21 + 42
   Ⓓ 78p − 21 + 42h

10. **5(6x + 17y − 9z) is equivalent to:**

   Ⓐ 30x + 82y − 45z
   Ⓑ 20x + 85y − 40z
   Ⓒ 30x + 85y − 45z
   Ⓓ 30x − 85y + 45z

11. **Which of the following equations represents 4(2 + 1c)? Choose all that apply.**

     Ⓐ 6 + 4c

     Ⓑ 6 + 5c

     Ⓒ 8 x 4c

     Ⓓ 8 + 4c

     Ⓔ (4 x 2) + (4 x 1c)

     Ⓕ (4 x 2) x (4 x 1c)

12. **[(8y) + (8y) + (8y)] ÷ 2 = _____ . Simplify the expression and write the answer in the box.**

Chapter 4

Lesson 7: Equations and Inequalities

You can scan the QR code given below or use the url to access additional EdSearch resources including videos and mobile apps related to *Equations and Inequalities*.

ed Search	Equations and Inequalities	
	URL	QR Code
	http://www.lumoslearning.com/a/6eeb5	

1. How many positive whole number solutions (values for x) does this inequality have?
   x ≤ 20

   Ⓐ 19
   Ⓑ 20
   Ⓒ 21
   Ⓓ Infinite

2. Which of the following correctly shows the number sentence that the following words describe? *17 is less than or equal to the product of 6 and q.*

   Ⓐ $17 \leq 6q$
   Ⓑ $17 \leq 6 - q$
   Ⓒ $17 < 6q$
   Ⓓ $17 \geq 6q$

3. Which of the following correctly shows the number sentence that the following words describe? *The quotient of d and 5 is 15.*

   Ⓐ $\dfrac{5}{d} = 15$

   Ⓑ $5d = 15$

   Ⓒ $\dfrac{d}{5} = 15$

   Ⓓ $d - 5 = 15$

4. Which of the following correctly shows the number sentence that the following words describe? *Three times the quantity u – 4 is less than 17*

   Ⓐ $3(u - 4) > 17$
   Ⓑ $3(u - 4) < 17$
   Ⓒ $3(u - 4) \leq 17$
   Ⓓ $3(u - 4) \geq 17$

5. Which of the following correctly shows the number sentence that the following words describe? *The difference between z and the quantity 7 minus r is 54.*

   Ⓐ $z - 7 - r = 54$
   Ⓑ $z + 7 - r = 54$
   Ⓒ $z + (7 - r) = 54$
   Ⓓ $z - (7 - r) = 54$

6. Which of the following correctly shows the number sentence that the following words describe? The square of the sum of 6 and b is greater than 10.

Ⓐ $(6 + b)^2 > 10$
Ⓑ $6^2 + b^2 > 10$
Ⓒ $(6 + b)^2 = 10$
Ⓓ $(6 + b)^2 < 10$

7. Which of the following correctly shows the number sentence that the following words describe? *16 less than the product of 5 and h is 21.*

Ⓐ $16 - 5h = 21$
Ⓑ $5h - 16 = 21$
Ⓒ $16 - (5 + h) = 21$
Ⓓ $16 < 5h + 21$

8. Which of the following correctly shows the number sentence that the following words describe? *8 times the quantity 2x – 7 is greater than 5 times the quantity 3x + 9.*

Ⓐ $8(2x) - 7 > 5(3x) + 9$
Ⓑ $8(2x - 7) \geq 5(3x + 9)$
Ⓒ $8(2x - 7) > 5(3x + 9)$
Ⓓ $8(2x - 7) < 5(3x + 9)$

9. A batting cage offers 8 pitches for a quarter. Raul has $1.50. Which expression could be used to calculate how many pitches Raul could get for his money?

Ⓐ $1.50 x 8
Ⓑ $1.50 ÷ 8
Ⓒ ($1.50 ÷ $0.25) x 8
Ⓓ ($1.50 ÷ $0.25)

10. For which of the following values of x is this inequality true?
$500 - 3x > 80$

Ⓐ x = 140
Ⓑ x = 150
Ⓒ x = 210
Ⓓ x = 120

11. Circle the answer that correctly represents "d" in this equation.

3d + 4 > 17

Ⓐ 5
Ⓑ 2
Ⓒ 4

12. Select all values that could correctly represent b in the equation.

3b + 2 < 15

Ⓐ 1
Ⓑ 2
Ⓒ 4
Ⓓ 5
Ⓔ 7

Chapter 4

Lesson 8: Modeling with Expressions

You can scan the QR code given below or use the url to access additional EdSearch resources including videos and mobile apps related to *Modeling with Expressions.*

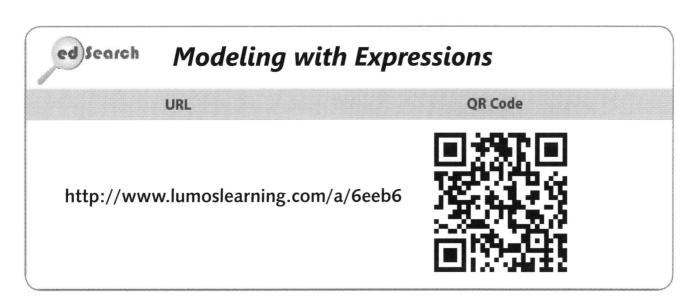

ed)Search	**Modeling with Expressions**	
URL		**QR Code**
http://www.lumoslearning.com/a/6eeb6		

1. Roula had 117 gumballs. Amy had x less than $\frac{1}{2}$ the amount that Roula had. Which expression shows how many gumballs Amy had?

   Ⓐ $117 - \frac{x}{2}$

   Ⓑ $(\frac{1}{2})(117) - x.$

   Ⓒ $117 - 2x$

   Ⓓ $2x + 117$

2. Benny earned $20.00 for weeding the garden. He also earned c dollars for mowing the lawn. Then he spent x dollars at the candy store. Which expression best represents this situation?

   Ⓐ $\$20 - c - x$

   Ⓑ $\$20 + c - x$

   Ⓒ $\$20 + c + x$

   Ⓓ $\$20 + \frac{x}{c}$

3. Clinton loves to cook. He makes a total of 23 different items. Clinton makes 6 different desserts, 12 appetizers, and x main courses. Which equation represents the total amount of food that Clinton cooked?

   Ⓐ $6 - 12 + x = 23$

   Ⓑ $6 + 12 + x = 23$

   Ⓒ $18 - x = 23$

   Ⓓ $6 + 12 - x = 23$

4. Simon has read 694 pages over the summer by reading 3 different books. He read 129 pages in the first book and he read 284 pages in the second book. Which equation shows how to figure out how many pages he read in the third book?

   Ⓐ $694 = 129 + 284 - y$

   Ⓑ $694 = 413 - y$

   Ⓒ $694 = 129 - 284 + y$

   Ⓓ $694 = 129 + 284 + y$

5. Jimmy had $45.00. He spent all of the money on a hat and a pair of jeans. He spent $19.00 on the pair of jeans and x dollars on the hat. Which of the following equations is true?

   Ⓐ $\$45.00 + x = \$19.00$

   Ⓑ $\$45.00 - x = \$19.00$

   Ⓒ $x - \$19.00 = \$45.00$

   Ⓓ $\$19.00 + 45.00 = x$

6. **Janie had 54 stamps. She gave away t stamps. She then got back twice as many as she had given away. Which expression shows how many stamps Janie has now?**

   Ⓐ $54 - t$
   Ⓑ $54 + t$
   Ⓒ $54 - 2t$
   Ⓓ $2t - 54$

7. **The library has 2,500 books. The librarian wants to purchase x more books for the library. The director decides to buy twice as many as the librarian requested. How many books will the library have if the director purchases the number of books he wants?**

   Ⓐ $2,500 + x$
   Ⓑ $2,500 + 2x$
   Ⓒ $2,500 - x$
   Ⓓ $2,500 - 2x$

8. **There are 24 boys and 29 girls (not including Claire) attending Claire's birthday party. Which equation shows how many cupcakes Claire needs to have so that everyone, including herself, will have a cupcake?**

   Ⓐ $24 - 29 = c$
   Ⓑ $24 + 29 = c$
   Ⓒ $24 + 30 = c$
   Ⓓ $24 + c = 29$

9. **Heidi collects dolls. She had 172 dolls in her collection. Heidi acquired x more dolls from a friend. She then bought twice as many dolls as she acquired from her friend from a yard sale. She now has 184 dolls in her collection. Which equation is true?**

   Ⓐ $172 + 3x = 184$
   Ⓑ $172 - x + 2x = 184$
   Ⓒ $172(3x) = 184$
   Ⓓ $172 - 3x = 184$

10. **Crystal grew 16 tomato plants. Each plant grew 10 tomatoes. She sold x of the tomatoes she had grown. Crystal has 54 tomatoes left for herself. Which equation is true?**

    Ⓐ $10(16 + x) = 54$
    Ⓑ $16(10 - x) = 54$
    Ⓒ $16 + x = 540$
    Ⓓ $160 - x = 54$

11. Circle the answer that represents the statement 43 is greater than q correctly.

(A) q > 43

(B) 43 + q

(C) 43 > q

12. Choose the box(es) that demonstrate that x is a number greater than 5. Choose all that apply.

(A) x < 5

(B) x > 5

(C) x + 5

(D) x - 5

(E) 5 < x

Chapter 4

Lesson 9: Solving One-Step Equations

You can scan the QR code given below or use the url to access additional EdSearch resources including videos and mobile apps related to *Solving One-Step Equations*.

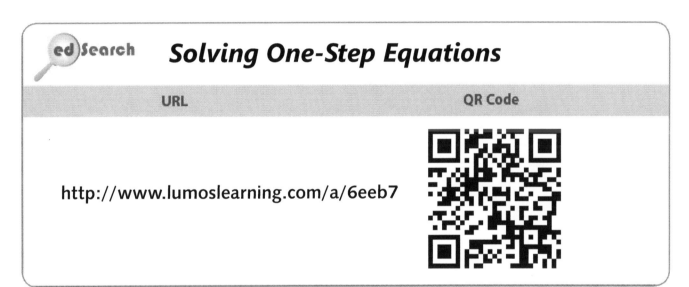

ed Search   *Solving One-Step Equations*

URL	QR Code
http://www.lumoslearning.com/a/6eeb7	

1. **Which of the following equations describes this function?**

X	Y
13	104
17	136
20	160
9	72

Ⓐ y = 18x
Ⓑ y = x + 4
Ⓒ y = x + 32
Ⓓ y = 8x

2. **What is the value of x?**

   − 7x = 56

Ⓐ x = −7
Ⓑ x = 8
Ⓒ x = −49
Ⓓ x = −8

3. **Does this table show a linear relationship between x and y?**

X	Y
13	169
15	225
12	144
	400
16	
7	
	64

Ⓐ yes
Ⓑ no
Ⓒ yes, but only when x is positive
Ⓓ yes, but only when y is a perfect square

4. **Find the value of z:** $\dfrac{z}{5} = 20$

Ⓐ 100
Ⓑ 4
Ⓒ 15
Ⓓ 25

5. **Find the value of y:** $\dfrac{y}{3} = 12$

    Ⓐ 9
    Ⓑ 15
    Ⓒ 36
    Ⓓ 4

6. **Find the value of p: 13 + p = 39**

    Ⓐ 3
    Ⓑ 26
    Ⓒ 507
    Ⓓ 52

7. **Find the value of *w*: 6*w* = 54**

    Ⓐ 48
    Ⓑ 60
    Ⓒ 324
    Ⓓ 9

8. **Find the value of *h*: *h* − 4 = 20**

    Ⓐ 24
    Ⓑ 16
    Ⓒ −80
    Ⓓ −5

9. **Find the value of p: 72 + p = 108**

    Ⓐ p = 30
    Ⓑ p = 36
    Ⓒ p = 180
    Ⓓ p = 40

10. **Find the value of n: 428 − n = 120**

    Ⓐ n = −548
    Ⓑ n = 308
    Ⓒ n = −308
    Ⓓ n = 548

11. Circle the answer that represents m correctly in the equation 4m = 16.

Ⓐ m = 4
Ⓑ m = 3
Ⓒ m = 12

12. Select the equations in which k = 8. Select all the correct answers.

Ⓐ 3(6 + k) = 42
Ⓑ ((4) 7) / k =14
Ⓒ 8k – 4 = 60
Ⓓ 7(k / 2) =35

Chapter 4

Lesson 10: Representing Inequalities

You can scan the QR code given below or use the url to access additional EdSearch resources including videos and mobile apps related to *Representing Inequalities*.

ed)Search	**Representing Inequalities**	
URL		**QR Code**
http://www.lumoslearning.com/a/6eeb8		

1. A second grade class raised caterpillars. They had 12 caterpillars. Less than half of the caterpillars turned into butterflies. Which inequality shows how many caterpillars turned into butterflies?

   Ⓐ x < 6
   Ⓑ x > 6
   Ⓒ x ≤ 6
   Ⓓ x ≥ 6

2. Elliot has at least 5 favorite foods. How many favorite foods could Elliot have?

   Ⓐ 4
   Ⓑ 2
   Ⓒ none
   Ⓓ an infinite number

3. Julie has a box full of crayons. Her box of crayons has 549 crayons and at least 8 of them are red. Which inequality represents how many crayons could be red?

   Ⓐ x ≥ 549
   Ⓑ 8 ≥ x ≥ 549
   Ⓒ 8 ≥ x
   Ⓓ 8 ≤ x ≤ 549

4. Five times a number is greater than that number minus 17 is represented as _____ .

   Ⓐ 5x > x − 17
   Ⓑ x + 5 > x − 17
   Ⓒ 5x < x − 17
   Ⓓ 5x > x + 17

5. "A number divided by five minus five is less than negative four" is represented as_____ .

   Ⓐ 5x − 5 < −4
   Ⓑ x/5 − 5 < −4
   Ⓒ x/5 − 5 > −4
   Ⓓ x/5 − 5 < 4

6. "Three times the sum of six times a number and three is less than 27." is represented as

   _____.

   Ⓐ 6x + 3 < 27
   Ⓑ 3(6)x + 3 > 27
   Ⓒ 3(6x + 3) < 27
   Ⓓ 6x + 3(3) < 27

7. **How would x > 3 be represented on a number line?**

   Ⓐ The number line would show an open circle over three with an arrow pointing to the left.
   Ⓑ The number line would show an open circle over three with an arrow pointing to the right.
   Ⓒ The number line would show a closed circle over three with an arrow pointing to the right.
   Ⓓ The number line would show a closed circle over three with an arrow pointing to the left.

8. **Amy and Joey each have jellybeans. The amount Amy has is 3 times the amount that Joey has. There are at least 44 jellybeans between them. Which inequality would help you figure out how many jellybeans Amy and Joey each have?**

   Ⓐ x + 3x ≥ 44
   Ⓑ 3x ≥ 44
   Ⓒ 3 + x ≥ 44
   Ⓓ x + 3x ≤ 44

9. **Sandra is a lawyer. She is working on x number of cases. She gets 8 more cases to work on. She now has more than 29 cases that she is working on. Which inequality could be used to figure out how many cases Sandra is working on?**

   Ⓐ 8x > 29
   Ⓑ x + 8 < 29
   Ⓒ x + 8 > 29
   Ⓓ x − 8 < 29

10. **There are 25 beehives on a farm. There are the same number of bees in each hive. The total number of bees on the farm is greater than 800. Which inequality could be used to figure out how many bees are in each hive?**

    Ⓐ 25/x > 800
    Ⓑ 25x < 800
    Ⓒ 25x > 800
    Ⓓ 25 + x > 800

11. **Circle the answer that represents the inequality shown on the number line below.**

    Ⓐ x ≥ 18
    Ⓑ x < 18
    Ⓒ x = 18

12. Choose the box that best represents the inequality on the line below.

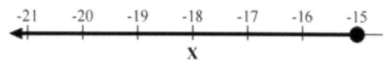

(A) x ≥ 15
(B) x ≥ -15
(C) x > -15
(D) x < -15
(E) x ≤ -15

13. A movie is rated PG13 meaning that one must be at least 13-years old to watch the movie. The sign in the lobby of the theater reads

PG13 Viewers
must be ≤ 13

Nami thinks the sign is wrong, but her friend Tai disagrees and finds nothing wrong with the sign. Who is correct and why?
Enter your answer in the box.

14. "A number divided by 5 is at most -23" is represented as _____.
Write the inequality and explain.

Chapter 4

Lesson 11: Quantitative Relationships

You can scan the QR code given below or use the url to access additional EdSearch resources including videos and mobile apps related to *Quantitative Relationships*.

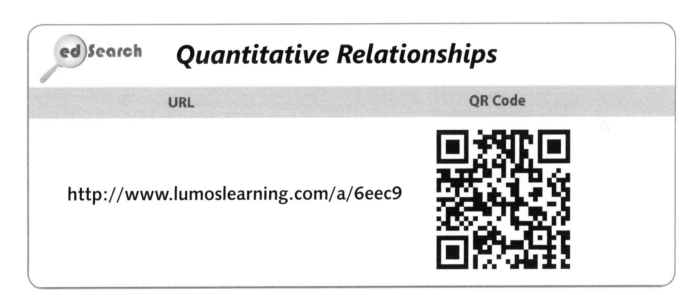

edSearch *Quantitative Relationships*

URL	QR Code
http://www.lumoslearning.com/a/6eec9	

1. Logan loves candy! He goes to the store and sees that the bulk candy is $0.79 a pound. Logan wants to buy p pounds of candy and needs to know how much money (m) he needs. Which equation would be used to figure out how much money Logan needs?

   Ⓐ m = 0.79 ÷ p
   Ⓑ m = 0.79(p)
   Ⓒ 0.79 = m(p)
   Ⓓ m = 0.79 + p

2. Logan loves candy! He goes to the store and sees that the bulk candy is $0.84 a pound. Logan wants to buy 3 pounds of candy. Using the equation m = 0.84(p), figure out how much money (m) Logan needs.

   Ⓐ $1.68
   Ⓑ $2.52
   Ⓒ $2.25
   Ⓓ $2.54

3. Norman is going on a road trip. He has to purchase gas so that he can make it to his first destination. Gas is $3.55 a gallon. Norman gets g gallons. Which equation would Norman use to figure out how much money (t) it cost to get the gas?

   Ⓐ t = g(3.55)
   Ⓑ t = g ÷ 3.55
   Ⓒ t = 3.55 ÷ g
   Ⓓ t = g + 3.55

4. Norman is going on a road trip. He has to purchase gas so that he can make it to his first destination. Gas is $3.58 a gallon. Norman needs to get 13 gallons. Using the expression t = g(3.58), figure out how much Norman will spend on gas.

   Ⓐ $46.15
   Ⓑ $39.54
   Ⓒ $46.45
   Ⓓ $46.54

5. Penny planned a picnic for her whole family. It has been very hot outside, so she needs a lot of lemonade to make sure no one is thirsty. There are 60 ounces in each bottle. Penny purchased b bottles of lemonade. She wants to figure out the total number of ounces (o) of lemonade she has. Which equation should she use?

   Ⓐ b = 60(o)
   Ⓑ 60 = o × b
   Ⓒ 60(b) = o
   Ⓓ 60 = b ÷ o

6. Ethan is playing basketball in a tournament. Each game lasts 24 minutes. Ethan has 5 games to play. Which general equation could he use to help him figure out the total number of minutes that he played? Let t = the total time, g = the number of games, and m = the time per game.

    Ⓐ t = g + m
    Ⓑ t = g(m)
    Ⓒ t = g − m
    Ⓓ t = g ÷ m

7. The Spencers built a new house. They want to plant trees around their house. They want to plant 8 trees in the front yard and 17 in the backyard. The trees that the Spencer's want to plant cost $46 each. Could they use the equation t = c(n) where t is the total cost, c is the cost per tree, and n is the number of trees purchased, to figure out the cost to purchase trees for both the front and the back yards?

    Ⓐ No, because the variables represent only two specific numbers that will never change.
    Ⓑ Yes, because the variables represent only two specific numbers that will never change.
    Ⓒ No, because the variables can be filled in with any number.
    Ⓓ Yes, because the variables can be filled in with any number.

8. Liz is a florist. She is putting together b bouquets for a party. Each bouquet is going to have f sunflowers in it. The sunflowers cost $3 each. Which equation can Liz use to figure out the total cost (c) of the sunflowers in the bouquets?

    Ⓐ c = 3(bf)
    Ⓑ c = bf ÷ 3
    Ⓒ c = 3b + f
    Ⓓ c = 3(b + f)

9. Liz is a florist. She is putting together 5 bouquets for a party. Each bouquet is going to have 6 sunflowers in it. The sunflowers cost $3 each. Using the equation c = 3(bf), figure out how much Liz will charge for the bouquets.

    Ⓐ $90
    Ⓑ $30
    Ⓒ $18
    Ⓓ $80

10. Hen B lays 4 times as many eggs as Hen A. (Let a = Number of eggs Hen A lays, b = Number of eggs Hen B lays)

Hen A	Hen B
2	8
4	16
7	28
11	44

Which equation represents this scenario?

Ⓐ $b = 4 \div a$
Ⓑ $b = 4 + a$
Ⓒ $b = 4a$
Ⓓ $b = 4a - 4$

11. Which of the following represent balloons that have a cost of $2.50 for a quantity of 10? Choose all that apply.

Ⓐ 20 balloons cost $1.25
Ⓑ 100 balloons $25.00
Ⓒ 30 balloons cost $7.50
Ⓓ 80 balloons cost $8.00

12. Sodas cost $1.25 at the vending machine. Complete the table to show the quantity and total cost of sodas purchased.

Day	Money Spent on Sodas	Sodas Purchased	Price per Soda
Monday		24	$1.25
Wednesday	$57.50		$1.25
Friday	$41.25		$1.25

End of Expressions & Equations

Chapter 4: Expressions & Equations

Answer Key
&
Detailed Explanations

Lesson 1: Whole Number Exponents

Question No.	Answer	Detailed Explanation
1	B	The base is 5. The exponent is 3. 5 is multiplied 3 times, or 5 X 5 X 5 = 125
2	C	The base is 2. Count the factors. There are 6. 6 is the exponent. $2 * 2 * 2 * 2 * 2 * 2 = 2^6$
3	D	The base is y. Count the factors. There are 4. 4 is the exponent. $y * y * y * y = y4$
4	A	Write the factors: 11 Since 11 is the only factor, $11^1 = 11$
5	C	2^2m^2 The first base is 2. Count the number of 2s. There are 2. 2 is the exponent, so part of the expression is 2^2 The second base is m. Count the number of ms. There are 2. 2 is the exponent, so part of the expression is m^2 The full expression is written as: 2^2m^2
6	C	$4^3 * 4^2 = 4 * 4 * 4 * 4 * 4 = 4^5$
7	C	We know that $a^m*a^n = a^{(m+n)}$. Therefore, $(b^2c)\ (bc^3) = b^3c^4$
8	B	We know that $a^m*a^n = a^{(m+n)}$. Therefore, $(n^4x^2)^3 = n^{12}x^6$
9	C	We know that $a^m/a^n = a^{(m-n)}$. Therefore, $7^4/7^2 = 7^2$
10	A	$[(3^5)(3^2)]^4 = 3^{28}$ Keep the base the same. 3 is the base. Add the exponents inside the brackets. 5 + 2 = 7. The expression becomes $[3^7]^4$. To simplify further, multiply the exponents (since the base has a power raised to a power.) $[3^7]^4 = 3^{7*4} = 3^{28}$
11	D & E	D. $10^2 = 10 \times 10 = 100$ E. $4^4 = 4 \times 4 \times 4 \times 4 = 256$
12	4096	$8^4 = 8 \times 8 \times 8 \times 8 = 4,096$

LumosLearning.com

Lesson 2: Expressions Involving Variables

Question No.	Answer	Detailed Explanation
1	A	Since 3(n + 7) is equal to 33, then (n + 7) must equal 11 (3 x 11 = 33). Therefore, n must equal 4, since 4 + 7 = 11.
2	B	A number joined to a variable through multiplication is a coefficient. 22 is the coefficient of x.
3	A	When n = 7, the expression becomes 5(7 - 5) = 5 (2) = 10.
4	B	When b = 26, 4b − 9 = 4(26) − 9 = 104 − 9 = 95
5	C	When n = −4, the expression becomes: = [5(-4) − 3(-4)] + 2(-4) = [−20 − (−12)] − 8 = [−20 + 12] − 8 = [−8] − 8 = −16 Alternative Solution: [5n-3n]+2n = 2n + 2n = 4n = 4*(-4) = -16
6	D	Four times a number n means to multiply the variable n by 4, 4n. is equal to means = the difference between a number and 10 means to write the subtraction as is, from left to right, so n − 10. Therefore, 4n = n − 10
7	B	First, combine like terms: 2y + 3y − y = 4y Then, substitute 2 for y: 4(2) =8
8	B	Substitute 2 for b and 3 for y: 2(2) − 4 + 6(3) = 4 − 4 + 18 = 0 + 18 = 18
9	D	a number n times 16 is equal to 48 a number n times 16: 16n is equal to: = 16n = 48 n = 3, since 16(3) = 48
10	C	When x = 7, 6x + 12 = 6(7) + 12 = 42 + 12 = 54
11	C	f - 12, The phrase "12 less than f" indicates than f is being reduced, or subtracted, by the number 12.
12	B & C	B and C, The order of the numbers should match the phrase.

Lesson 3: Identifying Expression Parts

Question No.	Answer	Detailed Explanation
1	C	$(4 - 2) \rightarrow$ The difference of 4 and 2. $6(4 - 2) \rightarrow$ The product of 6 and the difference of 4 and 2.
2	B	$(8 \div 2) \rightarrow$ The quotient of 8 and 2. $- 10 \rightarrow$ less 10 or 10 subtracted from. $(8 \div 2) - 10 \rightarrow$ 10 less than the quotient of 8 and 2.
3	D	A coefficient is the number multiplied by a variable. In this expression there are two variable terms, 2x and 9x. The coefficients are 2 and 9.
4	B	A coefficient is the number multiplied by a variable. In this expression there are three variable terms, $4a^2$, $9a$ and $-11b^2$. The coefficients are 4, 9, and -11. The value of the greatest coefficient is 9.
5	B	A factor is a term being multiplied by another term. In this expression we have four factors 4, $(6+8)$, 3 and $(2-5)$
6	C	$(5 \times \frac{1}{2}) \rightarrow$ The product of 5 and $\frac{1}{2}$ $4 \div (5 \times \frac{1}{2}) \rightarrow$ The quotient of 4 and the product of 5 and $\frac{1}{2}$
7	A	$(6 + 9) \rightarrow$ The sum of 6 and 9 or 6 plus 9 $- 4 \rightarrow$ less 4 or 4 subtracted from $(6 + 9) - 4 = 4$ subtracted from the sum of 6 and 9
8	C	A coefficient is the number multiplied by a variable. In this expression there are four variable terms, $8x^4$, $\frac{7}{8}x^3$, $-2x^2$ and x. The coefficients are $8, \frac{7}{8}, -2$ and 1. The value of the smallest coefficient is -2. Therefore the third term has the smallest coefficient.
9	D	The sum of 9 and $7 \rightarrow (9 + 7)$ The product of 5 and the sum of 9 and $7 \rightarrow 5(9 + 7)$
10	A	$(12 \div 4) \rightarrow$ The quotient of 12 and 4 $+ \rightarrow$ sum $[2 \times (-2)] \rightarrow$ the product of 2 and -2 $(12 \div 4) + [2 \times (-2)] \rightarrow$ The sum of the quotient of 12 and 4 and the product of 2 and -2.
11	A & B	A. $(2+1) + (2+1) + (2+1)$ B. $6 + 3$
12	A	A number or an expression added to itself is twice the number or expression.

Question No.	Answer		Detailed Explanation

Lesson 4: Evaluating Expressions

Question No.	Answer		Detailed Explanation
1	A	$y = 3x-13$	Original equation
		$y = 3(6)-13$	Substitute 6 for x
		$y = 18-13$	Multiply
		$y = 5$	Subtract
2	B	$y = \frac{1}{4}x \div 2$	Original equation
		$y = \frac{1}{4}(32) \div 2$	Substitute 32 for x
		$y = \frac{32}{4} \div 2$	Multiply
		$y = 8 \div 2$	Simplify fraction
		$y = 4$	Divide
3	D	$3a^2 - 7b$	Original equation
		$3(3)^2 - 7(-8)$	Substitute 3 for a and −8 for b
		$3(9) - 7(-8)$	Exponents
		$27 - 7(-8)$	Multiply
		$27 -(-56)$	Multiply
		$27+56$	Change to adding
		83	Add
4	C	$6v^3 + \frac{4}{5}w$	Original equation
		$6(-2)^3 + \frac{4}{5}(155)$	Substitute −2 for v and 155 for w
		$6(-8) + \frac{4}{5}(155)$	Exponents
		$-48 + \frac{4}{5}(155)$	Multiply
		$-48+124$	Multiply
		76	Add
5	B	$\frac{6}{d}-10c-c^4$	Original equation
		$\frac{6}{2}-10(-3)-(-3)^4$	Substitute −3 for c and 2 for d
		$\frac{6}{2}-10(-3) - (81)$	Exponents
		$3-10(-3) - (81)$	Divide
		$3-(-30) - (81)$	Multiply
		$3 + 30 - (81)$	Change to adding
		$33-(81)$	Add
		-48	Subtract

Question No.	Answer	Detailed Explanation	
6	C	$V = s^3$	Formula
		$V = s^3$	Substitute 2 for s
		$V = 8$ cm^3	Exponents
7	D	$A = l \times w$	Formula
		$A = 4.5 \times 7.3$	Substitute for l and w
		$A = 32.85$ ft^2	Multiply
8	B	$V = \pi r^2 h$	Formula
		$V = 3.14 \times (1.5)^2 \times 11$	Substitute the value for r and h (r=3/2=1.5)
		$V = 3.14 \times 2.25 \times 11$	Exponents
		$V = 77.715$	Multiply
		$V = 77.72$ in^3 rounding to two decimal places	
9	B	$A = s^2$	Formula
		$A = (\frac{3}{4})^2$	Substitute values
		$A = \frac{9}{16}$ m^2	Exponents
10	A	$V = \frac{1}{3} \text{ßh}$	Formula
		$V = \frac{1}{3}(10)(6)$	Substitute values
		$V = 20$ ft^3	Multiply
11	B	40, because 30 x 40 = 1200	
		Alternative Solution:	
		1200 / x = 30	
		x = 1200 / 30	
		x = 40	
12	B, C, & D	B. 56 − 7 = 49	
		C. 3(7) + 4 = 25	
		D. 7 x 7 x 7 = 343	

Question No.	Answer	Detailed Explanation

Lesson 5: Writing Equivalent Expressions

Question No.	Answer	Detailed Explanation
1	D	The expression, $3(n - 4)$, is equivalent because it has the same value as the original. The GCF (Greatest Common Factor) of 3 has been factored out from each term.
2	B	Here, the variable is the common factor and can be factored out $n(2 - 7)$. Then, simplify within the parentheses: $n(-5)$. Finally, use the Commutative Property to rewrite the expression, coefficient first: $-5n$.
3	B	$5y + 2z - 3y + z = 2y + 3z$ Combine the like terms to simplify: $5y + 2z - 3y + z = (5y - 3y) + (2z + z) = 2y + 3z$.
4	D	First use the Distributive Property to remove the parentheses: $8a + 9 - 3(a + 4) = 8a + 9 - 3a - 12$ Then, combine like terms: $8a + 9 - 3a - 12 = (8a - 3a) + (9 - 12) = 5a + (-3) = 5a - 3$
5	B	The Distributive Property states that a number outside of the parentheses should be used to multiply all numbers inside the parentheses. The inequality symbol should not change. The correct answer is $3q + 18 > 11$
6	D	Combine like terms.: $q + q + q + q + q = 5q$ Replace the simplified expression into the original inequality: $10 < 5q - 5$
7	B	Combine like terms in the expression. $u + u + u + u = 4u$ $-p + p + p = p$ That makes the equation $4u + p - r = 55$
8	B	The GCF of 36 and 12 is 12. The Distributive Property states that a number outside of the parentheses should be distributed to all numbers inside the parentheses. So, $36x - 12 = 108$ can be rewritten as $12(3x - 1) = 108$
9	B	The Distributive Property states that a number outside of the parentheses should be distributed to all numbers inside the parentheses. $5(3x + 2) = (5*3x) + (5*2) = 15x + 10$.
10	C	First use the Distributive Property to remove the parentheses: $5b - 9c - 2(4b + c) = 5b - 9c - 8b - 2c$ Then, combine like terms: $5b - 9c - 8b - 2c = (5b - 8b) + (-9c - 2c) = -3b + (-11c) = -3b - 11c$

Question No.	Answer	Detailed Explanation
11	(4 x 5) -3	(4 x 5) -3
12	A	8 + 6b The distributive property requires that 2 be multiplied by each quantity in parentheses, then the product of each is added. (2 x 4) + (2 x 3b) 8 + 6b

Question No.	Answer	Detailed Explanation

Lesson 6: Identifying Equivalent Expressions

Question No.	Answer	Detailed Explanation
1	B	$(\frac{5}{25})x$ and $(\frac{1}{5})x$ are equivalent because $\frac{5}{25}$ simplifies to $\frac{1}{5}$. The expressions will be equivalent even if a number is substituted for x.
2	C	7 + 21v and 7(1 + 3v) are equivalent because if you distribute 7 to 1 +3v you will get 7 + 21v. The expressions will be equivalent even if a number is substituted for v.
3	C	32p/2 and 16p are equivalent because if you divide 32p by 2 you get 16p. The expressions will be equivalent even if a number is substituted for p.
4	A	17(3m + 4) and 51m + 68 are equivalent because if you distribute 17 to 3m + 4 you will get 51m + 68. The expressions will be equivalent even if a number is substituted for m.
5	C	64k/4 and 16k are equivalent because if you divide 64k by 4 you will get 16k. The expressions will be equivalent even if a number is substituted for k.
6	A	25(23d − 4) and 575d − 100 are equivalent because if you distribute 25 to 23d − 4 you will get 575d − 100. The expressions will be equivalent even if a number is substituted for d.
7	C	(800 + 444y)/4 and 200 + 111y are equivalent because if you divide 800 + 444y by 4 you will get 200 + 111y. The expressions will be equivalent even if a number is substituted for y.
8	D	5(19 − 8y) and 95 − 40y are equivalent because if you distribute 5 to 19 − 8y you will get 95 − 40y. The expressions will be equivalent even if a number is substituted for y.
9	D	3(26p − 7 + 14h) and 78p − 21 + 42h are equivalent because if you distribute 3 to 26p − 7 + 14h you will get 78p − 21 + 42h. The expressions will be equivalent even if numbers are substituted for h and p.
10	C	5(6x + 17y − 9z) and 30x + 85y − 45z are equivalent because if you distribute 5 to 6x + 17y − 9z you will get 30x + 85y − 45z. The expressions will be equivalent even if x, y, and z are replaced with numbers.
11	D and E	The distributive property requires that 4 be multiplied by each value in parentheses then those products should be added together.
12	12 y	8y + 8y + 8y = 24y. Therefore given expression = 24y/2 = (24/2)y = 12y.

Lesson 7: Equations and Inequalities

Question No.	Answer	Detailed Explanation
1	B	x can be any whole number from 1 to 20, inclusive of 20.
2	A	"17 is less than or equal to" means $17 \leq$ "the product of 6 and q" means to multiply 6 and q, or 6q $17 \leq 6q$
3	C	"The quotient of d and 5" means to divide d by 5 "is 15" means "equals 15". $\frac{d}{5} = 15$
4	B	"Three times the quantity u – 4" means to multiply (u−4) by 3 → $3(u-4)$ "is less than 17" means < 17 $3(u-4) < 17$
5	D	"The difference between z and the quantity 7 minus r" means to find the difference between z and (7−r), so $z - (7-r)$ "is 54" means equals 54 So, $z - (7 - r) = 54$
6	A	"The square of the sum of 6 and b" means to square all of (6 + b), or $(6 + b)^2$ "is greater than 10" means "> 10" $(6 + b)^2 > 10$
7	B	"16 less than" means to "subtract 16 from some term" "the product of 5 and h" means to multiply 5 and h or "5h" "is 21" means "equals 21" $5h - 16 = 21$
8	C	"8 times the quantity 2x – 7" means to multiply 8 and $2x - 7$, which needs to be in parentheses (as a quantity), so $8(2x - 7)$ "is greater than" means "$>$" 5 times the quantity 3x + 9" means 5 multiplied by $3x + 9$, which needs to be in parentheses (as a quantity), so $5(3x+9)$ $8(2x - 7) > 5(3x + 9)$
9	C	To find how many quarters (or the equivalent of how many quarters) Raul has, you could calculate $1.50 divided by $0.25. Then, that amount of quarters would be multiplied by 8, the number of pitches purchased with each quarter. The final expression would read: ($1.50 ÷ $0.25) x 8

Question No.	Answer	Detailed Explanation
10	D	Solve to find x: $500 - 3x > 80$ First, subtract 500 from both sides $-3x > -420$ Next, divide both sides by -3. (Don't forget to switch the inequality sign when dividing a negative in an inequality) $x < 140$ So, $x = 120$ would work as a solution. To check: $500 - 3(120) = 500 - 360 = 140$, which is greater than 80.
11	A	5 because $3 \times 5 = 15$; $15 + 4$ is > 17.
12	A, B & C	1, 2, and 4 would complete the equation with a value < 15.

Lesson 8: Modeling with Expressions

Question No.	Answer	Detailed Explanation
1	B	Half of 117 can be expressed as (1/2)(117). x less than that is expressed as − x. (1/2)(117) − x.
2	B	Start with $20.00. Then add what he earned mowing the lawn (+c). Then subtract what he spent at the candy store (−x). The expression is $20 + c − x.
3	B	Clinton made a total of 23 items, so you know the expression has to equal 23. He made 6 desserts and 12 appetizers. You do not know how many main courses he made, so that is represented by x. 6 + 12 + x = 23
4	D	Simon read a total of 694 pages. Add the pages from the first book (129), the second book (284) and the third book (y) together. 694 = 129 + 284 + y
5	B	Subtracting the cost of the hat (x) from the total cost ($45.00) would leave the cost of the jeans ($19.00). $45.00 − x = $19.00.
6	B	Janie started with 54 stamps. Giving t stamps away means −t, so 54 − t. Then, Janie gets double t stamps back or + 2t. 54 − t + 2t. Simplified, the expression would be 54 + t.
7	B	The director wants to buy double of x books, which is 2x. Add that to the 2,500 existing books to create the expression 2,500 + 2x.
8	C	The total number of cupcakes is "c." There are 24 boys and 29 girls plus Claire (to make 30). Add all of the people together and equate it to "c." 24 + 30 = c
9	A	Heidi had 172 dolls to start with. She acquired x more so add x to 172. She then acquired 2x more, so add that to 172 also. 172 + x + 2x = 184 Simplify the equation to be: 172 + 3x = 184
10	D	Crystal had 16 plants and each grew 10 tomatoes. To figure out how many tomatoes Crystal had originally, multiply 16 x 10 = 160. Crystal sold x tomatoes, so subtract x from 160. Crystal has 54 tomatoes left. 160 − x = 54
11	C	Answer is 43 > q is the only choice that models a number "greater than" q.
12	B & E	x > 5 and 5 < x

Question No.	Answer	Detailed Explanation

Lesson 9: Solving One-Step Equations

Question No.	Answer	Detailed Explanation
1	D	Each time a number from x is multiplied by 8, the product is found in y. So, the equation is $y = 8x$.
2	D	To find the value of x, you must isolate it. Divide each side by −7. $-7x/-7 = 56/-7$. $x = -8$
3	B	Each value of y is the square of the corresponding x value. This is not a linear relationship.
4	A	$\frac{z}{5} = 20$ To find the value of z, you must isolate it. Multiply each side by 5/1 to cancel out the denominator and isolate the z. $z/5 * 5/1 = z$ $20 * 5/1 = 100$ so, $z = 100$
5	C	$\frac{y}{3} = 12$ To find the value of y, you must isolate it. Multiply by 3 on each side to isolate the y. $y/3*(3/1) = 12(3/1)$ $y = 36$
6	B	To find the value of p, you must isolate it. Subtract 13 from both sides to isolate the variable. $13 + p - 13 = 39 - 13$ $p = 26$
7	D	To find the value of w, you must isolate it. Divide each side by the coefficient, 6, to isolate the variable. $6w/6 = 54/6$ $w = 9$
8	A	To find the value of x, you must isolate it. Add 4 to both sides. $h - 4 = 20$ $h - 4 + 4 = 20 + 4$ $h = 24$

Question No.	Answer	Detailed Explanation
9	B	To find the value of p, you must first isolate it. Do that by subtracting 72 from both sides. 72 + p −72 = 108 −72 p = 36
10	B	To find the value of n, you must isolate it. Subtract 428 from both sides. 428 − n − 428 = 120 − 428 −n = −308 Divide both sides by −1 n = 308
11	A	To find the value of m, you must isolate it. Divide both the sides by 4. 4m / 4 = 16 / 4 m = 4
12	A & C	A. 3(6 + k) = 42 (3 x 6) + (3 x 8) = 42 18 + 24 = 42 C. 8k − 4 = 60 8(8) − 4 = 60 64 − 4 = 60

Question No.	Answer	Detailed Explanation

Lesson 10: Representing Inequalities

1	A	Half of 12 is 6. Less than 6 caterpillars turned into butterflies. That means that $x < 6$.
2	D	Elliot has at least 5 different favorite foods. That means that he has more than 5 favorite foods. He could have an infinite number of favorite foods because there is no constraint on the number of favorite foods he could have.
3	D	There can be no more than 549 red crayons because that is the maximum number of crayons in the box. You know there are at least 8 red crayons, which means that x is greater than or equal to 8 and less than or equal to 549. $8 \leq x \leq 549$
4	A	"Five times a number" is represented as 5x. "Is greater than" is represented as $>$. "That number minus 17" is represented as $x - 17$. $5x > x - 17$
5	B	"A number divided by 5" is represented as x/5. "Minus five" is represented as $- 5$. "Is less than" is represented as $<$. "Negative four" is represented as -4. $x/5 - 5 < -4$
6	C	"A number times six plus three" is represented as $6x + 3$. Three times that is represented as $3(6x + 3)$. "Is less than" is represented as $<$. $3(6x + 3) < 27$
7	B	An open circle means that the number the circle is over is not included in the answer. An arrow pointing to the right means "greater than". The number line would show an open circle over three with an arrow pointing to the right.
8	A	The number of jellybeans that Joey has is represented as x. Amy has three times that many so that is represented as 3x. Together they have at least 44. That means that their jellybeans added together are at least 44, so that is represented as x + 3x. At least means that they could have 44 or more than 44 so that is represented as $\geq$ $x + 3x \geq 44$

Question No.	Answer	Detailed Explanation
9	C	The number of cases that Sandra has is represented as x. The 8 more she gets is represented as x + 8. She has more than 29, so that is represented as > 29 x + 8 > 29
10	C	The number of bees in each hive is represented as x. There are the same number of bees in all 25 beehives. The total number of bees is represented as 25x. The total number of bees on the farm is greater than 800. Greater than is represented as > 800. 25x > 800
11	A	Closed circle represents "Greater than or equal to" or "less than or equal to" on the number line. An arrow to the right represents "greater than". Answer is $x \geq 18$.
12	E	Closed circle represents "Greater than or equal to" or "less than or equal to" on the number line. An arrow to the left represents "less than". $x \leq -15$
13		Nami is correct, the sign is wrong. To be at least 13 years old means to be 13 years old or older. Hence the correct inequality symbol is $\geq$ and not $\leq$. The arrow points toward the smaller number. In this case the smaller number is 13.
14		"A number" is represented as x. "Divided by 5" is represented as $\frac{x}{5}$. "Is at most" means that it could be -23 or less than -23, so that is represented as $\leq$ $\frac{x}{5} \leq -23$

Question No.	Answer	Detailed Explanation
	**Lesson 11: Quantitative Relationships**

Question No.	Answer	Detailed Explanation
1	B	"m" represents the amount of money that Logan needs. "p" represents the number of pounds that Logan buys. The amount of money Logan needs is found by multiplying the cost of the candy by the number of pounds that Logan buys. m = 0.79(p)
2	B	m = $0.84(3) m = $2.52
3	A	"t" represents the total amount Norman spent. "g" represents the number of gallons that Norman purchased. To find the total amount that Norman spent, multiply the price of the gas by the total number of gallons that Norman purchased. t = g(3.55)
4	D	t = 13 gallons ($3.58) t = 13(3.58) t = 46.54 $46.54
5	C	"b" represents the number of bottles of lemonade "o" represents the total number of ounces of lemonade To find out the total number of ounces of lemonade that Penny purchased, multiply the number of bottles (b) by the number of ounces in each bottle, 60. 60(b) = o
6	B	"t" represents the total number of minutes Ethan played "g" represents the number of games "m" represent the number of minutes in each game To find out the total number of minutes Ethan played, multiply the number of games by the number of minutes in each game. t = g(m)
7	D	The equation t = c(n) can be used with any numbers. The equation has the number of trees and the cost of one tree as variables. Those quantities, no matter what they are, when multiplied together will always equal the total cost.
8	A	"c" represents the total cost "b" represents the number of bouquets "f" represents the number of sunflowers To find the total cost, multiply the number of bouquets by the number of sunflowers by the price of the sunflowers. c = 3(bf)

Question No.	Answer	Detailed Explanation
9	A	$c = 3(bf)$ $c = 3(6)(5)$ $c = 90$ $90
10	C	The number of eggs that Hen B lays depends on the number of eggs that Hen A lays. Hen B lays 4 times more than Hen A. That is represented as 4a $b = 4a$
11	B & C	B. 100 balloons equal 10 packs of 10 $2.50 x 10 quantity = $25.00 C. 30 balloons equal 3 packs of 10 $2.50 x 3 = $7.50
12		(table below)

Day	Money Spent on Sodas	Sodas Purchased	Price per Soda
Monday	**$30.00**	24	$1.25
Wednesday	$57.50	**46**	$1.25
Friday	$41.25	33	$1.25

m = $30.00
24 x $1.25 = $30
w = 46 sodas
$57.50 / $1.25 = 46
f = 33 sodas
$41.25/ $1.25 = 33

Chapter 5: Geometry

Lesson 1: Area

You can scan the QR code given below or use the url to access additional EdSearch resources including videos and mobile apps related to *Area*.

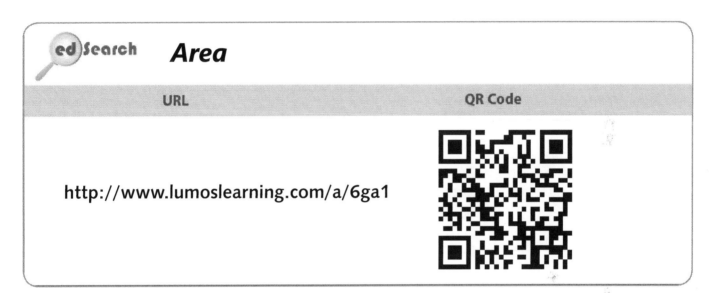

ed)Search **Area**	
URL	QR Code
http://www.lumoslearning.com/a/6ga1	

1. **What is the area of the figure below?**

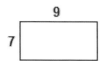

Ⓐ 16 square units
Ⓑ 63 square units
Ⓒ 32 square units
Ⓓ 45 square units

2. **What is the area of the figure below?**

Ⓐ 12 square units
Ⓑ 24 square units
Ⓒ 18 square units
Ⓓ 36 square units

3. **What is the area of the figure below? (Assume that the vertical height of the parallelogram is 3 units.)**

Ⓐ 28 square units
Ⓑ 12 square units
Ⓒ 14 square units
Ⓓ 21 square units

4. The figure shows a small square inside a larger square. What is the area of the shaded portion of the figure below?

Ⓐ 64 square units
Ⓑ 48 square units
Ⓒ 16 square units
Ⓓ 80 square units

5. What is the area of the figure below?

Ⓐ 14 square units
Ⓑ 28 square units
Ⓒ 49 square units
Ⓓ 21 square units

6. What is the area of the figure below? (Assume that the vertical height of the triangle is 2.8 units)

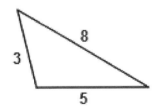

Ⓐ 15 square units
Ⓑ 7 square units
Ⓒ 14 square units
Ⓓ 40 square units

7. What is the area of the figure below?

5

12

Ⓐ 60 square units
Ⓑ 17 square units
Ⓒ 34 square units
Ⓓ 7 square units

8. What is the area of the figure shown below? The vertical height is 6 units.

19

7

Ⓐ 133 square units
Ⓑ 26 square units
Ⓒ 52 square units
Ⓓ 114 square units

9. What is the area of the gray part of the squares below?.

17   9

Ⓐ 289 square units
Ⓑ 81 square units
Ⓒ 208 square units
Ⓓ 370 square units

10. What is the area of a triangle with a base of 20 feet and a vertical height of 40 feet?

Ⓐ A = 200 square ft.
Ⓑ A = 800 square ft.
Ⓒ A = 400 square ft.
Ⓓ A = 600 square ft.

11. Calculate the area of the triangle shown below and write the answer in the box.

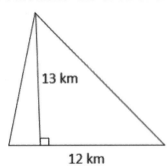

13 mm

17 mm

mm²

12. Calculate the area of the triangle shown. Write the answer in the box given below.

13 km

12 km

km²

13. George and Maggie were completing their homework together. One problem asked to find the area of a triangle. Below are George's and Maggie's work.

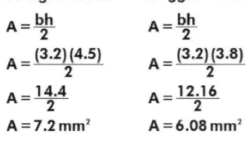

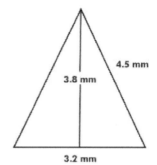

Whose answer is correct? Explain your reasoning.

Chapter 5

Lesson 2: Surface Area and Volume

You can scan the QR code given below or use the url to access additional EdSearch resources including videos and mobile apps related to *Surface Area and Volume*.

ed Search   *Surface Area and Volume*

URL	QR Code
http://www.lumoslearning.com/a/6ga2	

1. **How many rectangular faces would a trapezoidal prism have?**

    Ⓐ two
    Ⓑ four
    Ⓒ six
    Ⓓ zero

2. **Which of the following statements is true of a rhombus?**

    Ⓐ A rhombus is a parallelogram.
    Ⓑ A rhombus is a quadrilateral.
    Ⓒ A rhombus is equilateral.
    Ⓓ All of the above are true.

3. **A cube has a volume of 1,000 cm³. What is its surface area?**

    Ⓐ 100 square cm
    Ⓑ 60 square cm
    Ⓒ 600 square cm
    Ⓓ It cannot be determined.

4. **A solid figure is casting a square shadow. The figure could <u>not</u> be a _____ .**

    Ⓐ rectangular prism
    Ⓑ cylinder
    Ⓒ pentagonal pyramid
    Ⓓ hexagonal prism

5. **Which of the following solid figures has the most flat surfaces?**

    Ⓐ a cube
    Ⓑ a triangular prism
    Ⓒ a hexagonal prism
    Ⓓ a pentagonal pyramid

6. **Calculate the surface area of the box shown below.**

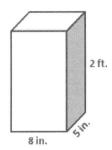

8 in.   5 in.   2 ft.

Ⓐ 132 square inches
Ⓑ 80 square inches
Ⓒ 704 square inches
Ⓓ 352 square inches

7. **Complete the following statement.**
   A hexagon must have _____.

Ⓐ 6 sides and 6 angles
Ⓑ 8 sides and 8 angles
Ⓒ 10 sides and 10 angles
Ⓓ 7 sides and 7 angles

8. **A single marble tile measures 25 cm by 20 cm. How many tiles will be required to cover a floor with dimensions 2 meters by 3 meters?**

Ⓐ 320 tiles
Ⓑ 240 tiles
Ⓒ 180 tiles
Ⓓ 120 tiles

9. **Calculate the volume of the box shown below.**

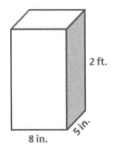

8 in.   5 in.   2 ft.

Ⓐ 80 cubic inches
Ⓑ 960 cubic inches
Ⓒ 800 cubic inches
Ⓓ None of the above

10. **What is the surface area of a rectangular box with dimensions 4 cm, 6 cm, and 10 cm?**

   Ⓐ 248 square cm
   Ⓑ 240 square cm
   Ⓒ 124 square cm
   Ⓓ 224 square cm

11. **What is the volume of a rectangular prism that has a length of 10 cm, a width of 5 cm, and a height of 2 cm? Circle the correct answer choice.**

   Ⓐ V = 50 cubic cm
   Ⓑ V = 17 cubic cm
   Ⓒ V = 10 cubic cm
   Ⓓ V = 100 cubic cm

12. **Determine the volume of the prism shown. Write your answer in the box given below.**

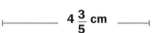

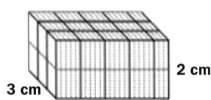

   cm³

Chapter 5

Lesson 3: Coordinate Geometry

You can scan the QR code given below or use the url to access additional EdSearch resources including videos and mobile apps related to *Coordinate Geometry*.

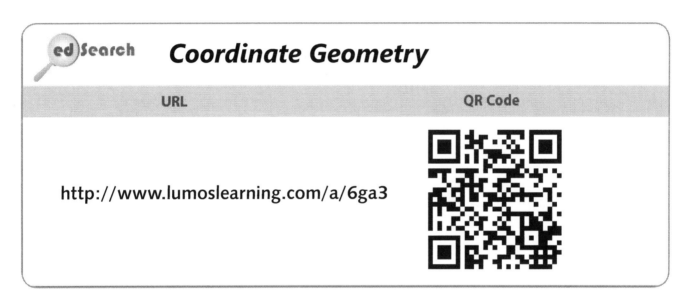

ed Search	***Coordinate Geometry***
URL	**QR Code**
http://www.lumoslearning.com/a/6ga3	

1. **The points A (0, 0), B (5, 0), C (6, 2), D (5, 5), and E (0, 5) are plotted in a coordinate grid. Describe the angles in pentagon ABCDE.**

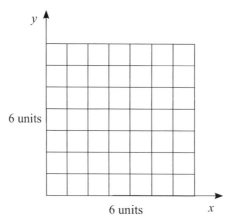

  Ⓐ 2 right angles and 3 obtuse angles
  Ⓑ 2 right angles, 1 obtuse angle, and 2 acute angles
  Ⓒ 3 right angles and 2 obtuse angles
  Ⓓ 2 right angles, 2 acute angles, and 1 obtuse angle

2. **The corners of a shape are located at (1,2), (5,2), (2,3) and (4,3) in a coordinate grid. What type of shape is it?**

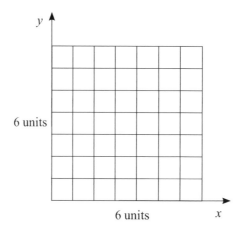

  Ⓐ square
  Ⓑ parallelogram
  Ⓒ rhombus
  Ⓓ trapezoid

3. **Which of the following graphs shows a 180-degree clockwise rotation about the origin?**

Ⓐ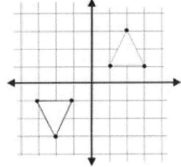

Ⓑ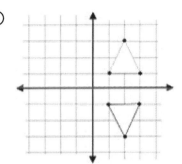

Ⓒ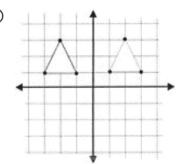

Ⓓ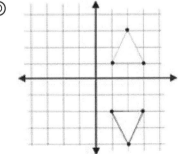

4. **Identify tx = 2y + 3, when y = 2.**

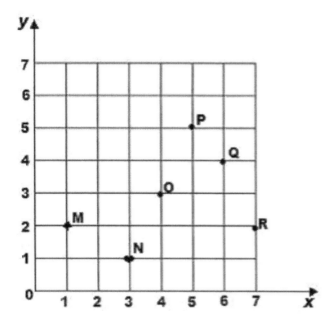

 Ⓐ Point M
 Ⓑ Point N
 Ⓒ Point R
 Ⓓ Point Q

5. **Which figure is formed when you draw straight line segments between the following points (in the order they are listed)? (2, −13), (2, 1), (8, 1), (8, 5), (2, 5), (2, 10), (−2, 10), (−2, 5), (−8, 5), (−8, 1), (−2, 1), (−2, −13)**

 Ⓐ star
 Ⓑ cross
 Ⓒ heart
 Ⓓ boat

6. **You are looking for a point on the line: y = 10 − 2x. You know that x = −1. What does y equal?**

 Ⓐ 10
 Ⓑ 8
 Ⓒ 12
 Ⓓ −2

7. **Assume a function has the rule y = 2x. Which grid shows the ordered pair formed when x = 3?**

Ⓐ
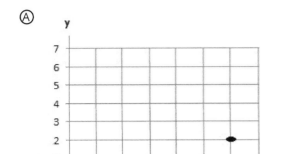

Ⓑ
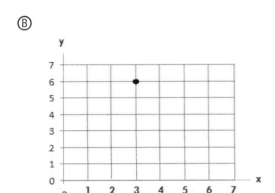

Ⓒ
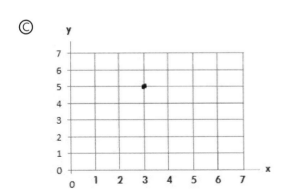

Ⓓ None of the above

8. **Which equation matches this graph?**

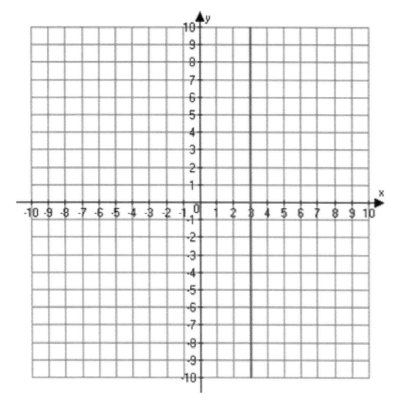

(A) y = 3
(B) x = 3
(C) y = 0
(D) x = −3

9. **What ordered pair would fit in this equation?**

   y = x − 3

   (A) (4, 0)
   (B) (0, 4)
   (C) (4, 1)
   (D) (1, 4)

10. **The upper left region of the coordinate plane is Quadrant** _____

   (A) IV
   (B) I
   (C) II
   (D) III

11. What is the area of this polygon? Write your answer in the box given below.

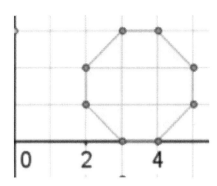

square units

12. What is the area of the rectangle. Write your answer in the box given below.

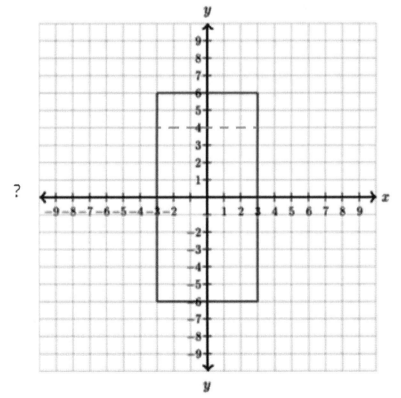

square units

Chapter 5

Lesson 4: Nets

You can scan the QR code given below or use the url to access additional EdSearch resources including videos and mobile apps related to *Nets*.

URL	QR Code
http://www.lumoslearning.com/a/6ga4	

1. Identify the solid given its net:

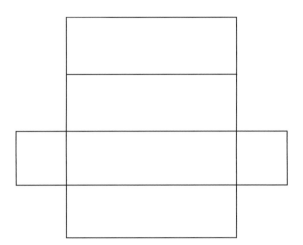

   Ⓐ Rectangular prism
   Ⓑ Cube
   Ⓒ Triangular prism
   Ⓓ Sphere

2. Identify the solid given its net:

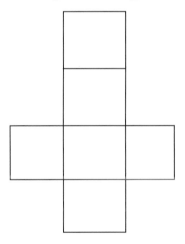

   Ⓐ Cube
   Ⓑ Sphere
   Ⓒ Rectangular prism
   Ⓓ Square pyramid

3. **Identify the solid given its net:**

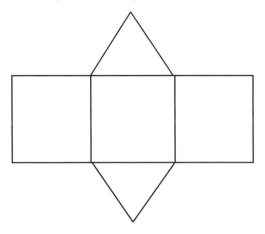

   Ⓐ Rectangular prism
   Ⓑ Cube
   Ⓒ Triangular prism
   Ⓓ Sphere

4. **Identify the solid given its net:**

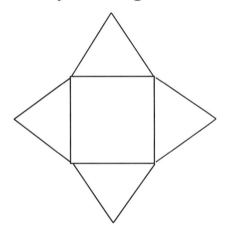

   Ⓐ Cube
   Ⓑ Sphere
   Ⓒ Rectangular prism
   Ⓓ Square pyramid

5. Identify the solid given its net:

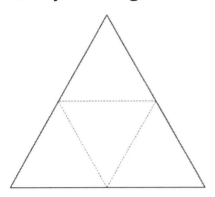

Ⓐ Cube
Ⓑ Sphere
Ⓒ Rectangular prism
Ⓓ Triangular pyramid

6. Identify the solid given its net:

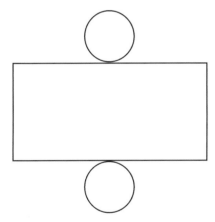

Ⓐ Cube
Ⓑ Sphere
Ⓒ Cylinder
Ⓓ Square pyramid

7. **Identify the solid given its net:**

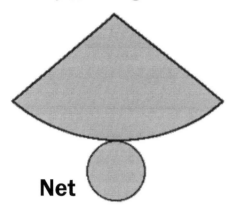

Ⓐ Cube
Ⓑ Cone
Ⓒ Cylinder
Ⓓ Square pyramid

8. **The diagram below represents the net of a solid figure. Find the surface area given L = 4 in, W = 4 in, H = 12 in.**

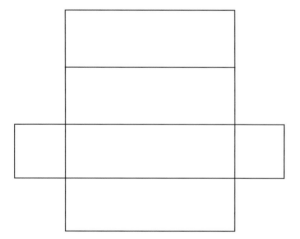

Ⓐ 228 square ft.
Ⓑ 224 square in.
Ⓒ 448 square in.
Ⓓ 112 square in.

9. **Identify the solid, given its net:**

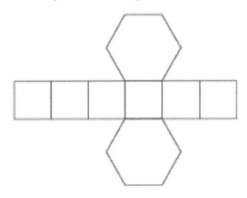

(A) Sphere
(B) Cone
(C) Hexagonal prism
(D) Hexagonal pyramid

10. **Identify the number of faces, edges and vertices in a rectangular pyramid.**

(A) Faces = 5, Vertices = 6, Edges = 9
(B) Faces = 4, Vertices = 4, Edges = 6
(C) Faces = 6, Vertices = 8, Edges = 12
(D) Faces = 5, Vertices = 5, Edges = 8

11. **Use a net or formula to find the surface area of the figure. The length is 5, the width is 4 and the height is 2. Write your answer in the box given below.**

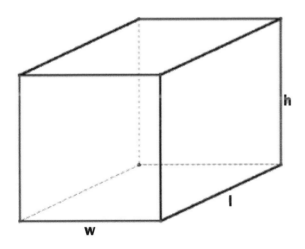

12. Use a net or formula to find the surface area of the figure. Length is 2, width is 3, and height is 4. Circle the correct answer choice.

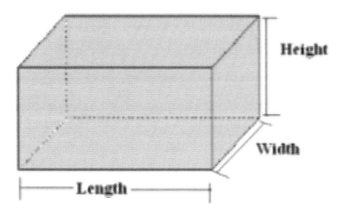

- Ⓐ 52 square units
- Ⓑ 42 square units
- Ⓒ 32 square units
- Ⓓ 22 square units

13. Identify the number of faces, edges and vertices in a hexagonal prism. Circle the correct answer choice.

- Ⓐ Faces = 8, Vertices = 10, Edges = 16
- Ⓑ Faces = 8, Vertices = 12, Edges = 20
- Ⓒ Faces = 8, Vertices = 12, Edges = 18
- Ⓓ Faces = 8, Vertices = 10, Edges = 18

End of Geometry

Chapter 5: Geometry

Answer Key
&
Detailed Explanations

Lesson 1: Area

Question No.	Answer	Detailed Explanation
1	B	Area of a rectangle = length x width. A = 9 x 7 A = 63 units^2
2	D	Area of a square = (length of side)^2. A = 6^2 A = 36 units^2
3	D	Area of a parallelogram = base x height. A= 7 x 3 A = 21 units^2
4	B	First find the area of the larger square. Then find the area of the smaller square. Use the formula: A = (length of side)^2 to find the area of both squares. A_{large} = 8 × 8 = 64 A_{small} = 4 × 4 = 16 Subtract the area of the smaller square from the larger square to find the area of the shaded portion (64 − 16 = 48).
5	C	Area of a square A = (length of side)^2 A= 7 x 7 A= 49 units^2
6	B	Area of a triangle = (1/2)bh A= $(\frac{1}{2})$ (5*2.8) A= $(\frac{1}{2})$ (14) A = 7 units^2
7	A	A=bh A= 5 x 12 A= 60 units^2
8	D	A= bh (where h is the vertical height of the parallelogram) A= 19 x 6 A= 114 units^2
9	C	Area of a square = (length of side)^2 Area of the larger square is 17*17 = 289 units^2 Area of the smaller square is 9*9 = 81 units^2 To find the area of the shaded portion, subtract the area of the smaller square from the area of the larger square: 289 − 81 = 208

Question No.	Answer	Detailed Explanation
10	C	The formula for the area of a triangle is: $A = (\frac{1}{2})bh$ $a = (\frac{1}{2})(20)(40)$ $a = (\frac{1}{2})(800)$ $a = 400$ sq. ft.
11	110.5 mm^2	For a triangle, Area = ½ (base x height) b = 17 mm h = 13 mm So, ½ (17 x 13) = area ½ (221) = 110.5 mm^2
12	78 km^2	Area = ½ (base x height) b = 12 km h = 13 km So, ½ (12 x 13) = area ½ (156) = 78 km^2
13		Maggie's answer is correct. The height of a triangle is perpendicular to its base. George used the side of the triangle as the triangle's height but the side is not perpendicular to the base of 3.2mm. Maggie, however, did use the height, which is 3.8 mm, as it is perpendicular to the base.

Question No.	Answer	Detailed Explanation

Lesson 2: Surface Area and Volume

1	B	A prism has rectangular faces connecting the two bases. A trapezoid has four sides, so four rectangular faces are on a trapezoidal prism.
2	D	A rhombus is a parallelogram that is a quadrilateral and is equilateral.
3	C	Since the volume of a cube is found using the formula: $V = $ (side length)^3, the length of each side of this cube would be 10 [$V = $ (10)(10)(10)]. The surface area of a cube is found by finding the area of one face: $A = $ (side)^2, then multiplying by 6, since there are 6 faces, so 6(side)^2. $6(10)^2 = 6(10)(10) = 6(100) = 600$
4	C	A pentagonal prism has 5 sides so it would not cast a square shadow.
5	C	A hexagonal prism would have a total of 8 faces. A cube has 6, a triangular prism has 5, and a pentagonal pyramid has 6.
6	C	First convert 2 feet to inches. There are 12 inches per foot so 2 feet is $12 * 2 = 24$ inches. The given figure is a cuboid or a rectangular prism which has six rectangular surfaces. Area of a rectangle = length x breadth. Therefore total S.A. $= 2(L_1W_1) + 2(L_2W_2) + 2(L_3W_3)$ where L_1W_1 are the dimensions of the top and bottom faces of the prism; L_2W_2 are the dimensions of the front and back faces of the prism and L_3W_3 are the dimensions of the side faces of the prism. Replace the variables with the appropriate values: S.A. $= 2(5*8) + 2(8*24) + 2(5*24)$ S.A. $= 2(40) + 2(192) + 2(120)$ S.A. $= 80 + 384 + 240$ S.A. $= 704$ square inches
7	A	A hexagon is a shape with 6 angles and 6 sides.
8	D	First, convert meters into centimeters to standardize the measurement units. 1 meter = 100 centimeters, so 2 meters = 200 centimeters and 3 meters = 300 centimeters. To find how many tiles will be needed across, divide $\frac{300}{25} = 12$ To find how many tiles will be needed down, divide $\frac{200}{20} = 10$ Then multiply the number of tiles needed across the floor by the number of times needed down the floor. $12*10 = 120$ tiles.

Question No.	Answer	Detailed Explanation
9	B	To find the volume of a rectangular prism, use the following formula: $V = LWH$ Substitute the appropriate values for the variables. Then simplify. First convert 2 feet to inches. There are 12 inches per foot so 2 feet is $12 * 2 = 24$ inches. $V = (8)(5)(24)$ $V = (40)(24)$ $V = 960$ cubic inches
10	A	To find the surface area, use the following formula: $S.A. = 2(L_1W_1) + 2(L_2W_2) + 2(L_3W_3)$ Where L_1W_1 represent the top and bottom of the prism L_2W_2 represent the front and back faces of the prism L_3W_3 represent the side faces of the prism. Replace the variables with the appropriate values: $S.A. = 2(4*6) + 2(4*10) + 2(6*10)$ $S.A. = 2(24) + 2(40) + 2(60)$ $S.A. = 48 + 80 + 120$ $S.A. = 248$ sq. cm.
11	D	$V = LWH$ $V = (10)(5)(2)$ $V = 50(2)$ $V = 100$ cubic cm
12	$27\frac{3}{5}$ cm³	$V = lwh$ cm³ $= (4\frac{3}{5})(3)(2)$ $V = (\frac{23}{5})(3)(2)$ $V = \frac{23 \times 3 \times 2}{5} = \frac{138}{5} = 27\frac{3}{5}$ cm³

Question No.	Answer	Detailed Explanation

Lesson 3: Coordinate Geometry

1	A	When the points are connected, Angles A and E are right angles and Angles B, C, and D are all obtuse angles.
2	D	When the points are correctly connected, a trapezoid is created.
3	A	A 180-degree clockwise rotation about the origin will cause the top of the triangle to point to the bottom, and also the shape to shift from Quadrant I to Quadrant III.
4	C	$x = 2y + 3$, when $y = 2$ Substitute 2 for y. $x = 2(2) + 3$ $x = 4 + 3$ $x = 7$ This makes the ordered pair (7,2), which corresponds to point R.
5	B	 When all points are correctly plotted, a cross is formed.
6	C	To determine the value of y, substitute the given value of x into the equation. $y = 10 - 2x$. If $x = -1$, then $y = 10 - 2(-1)$ $y = 10 - (-2)$ $y = 12$
7	B	To determine the value of y, substitute the given value of x into the equation. $y = 2x$. If $x = 3$, then $y = 2(3)$ $y = 6$ giving you the coordinate (3,6)
8	B	The equation, $x = 3$, will match the graph above, because for any given y coordinates, x will always be 3.

Question No.	Answer	Detailed Explanation
9	C	To determine what ordered pair would fit, substitute each x-coordinate and solve for the y-coordinate. A) (4, 0): x=4 so y = 4 − 3 = 1;The y-coordinate is 0 not 1 so this ordered pair does not fit. B) (0, 4): x=0 so y = 0 − 3 = −3;The y-coordinate is 4 not −3 so this ordered pair does not fit. C) (4,1): x=4 so y = 4 − 3 = 1; since the y-coordinate is also 1 this ordered pair fits. D) (1, 4): x=4 so y = 1 − 3 = −2;The y-coordinate is 4 not −2 so this ordered pair does not fit. Answer C is the only ordered pair that fits.
10	C	The Quadrants move counter clockwise from I to IV. The upper left region would be Quadrant II.
11	7 square units.	7 square units. There are 5 whole square units. There are 4 units that are right triangles, for a total of 2 whole squares. 5 + 2 = 7 square units.
12	72 square units	72 square units. 6 units along the x-axis multiplied by 12 units along the y-axis equals. 72 total square units.

Question No.	Answer	Detailed Explanation

Lesson 4: Nets

Question No.	Answer	Detailed Explanation
1	A	When the exposed edges are connected a rectangular prism will be formed.
2	A	When the exposed edges are connected a cube will be formed.
3	C	When the exposed edges are connected a triangular prism will be formed.
4	D	When the exposed edges are connected a square pyramid will be formed.
5	D	When the exposed edges are connected a triangular pyramid will be formed.
6	C	When the exposed edges are connected a cylinder will be formed.
7	B	When the exposed edges are connected a cone will be formed.
8	B	This net represents a rectangular prism. The surface area of a rectangular prism = 2(l*w + l*h + w*h) = 2(4*4 + 4*12 + 4*12) = 2(16 + 48 + 48) = 2(112) = 224 square in.
9	C	The hexagon ends, attached by six rectangular faces, create a hexagonal prism.
10	D	There are 5 faces, 5 vertices, and 8 edges in a rectangular pyramid.
11	C	To find the surface area, find the area of each side using the net S.A. = (5*4) + (5*4) + (4*2) + (4*2) + (5*2) + (5*2) = = 20 + 20 + 8 + 8 + 10 + 10 = 76 square units

Question No.	Answer	Detailed Explanation
12	A	Find the area of each face and add all the areas together in order to find the surface area: (2*3) + (2*3) + (3*4) + (3*4) + (2*4) + (2*4) = 52 units^2
13	C	There are 8 faces, 12 vertices, and 18 edges in a hexagonal prism.

Chapter 6:
Statistics & Probability

Lesson 1: Statistical Questions

You can scan the QR code given below or use the url to access additional EdSearch resources including videos and mobile apps related to *Statistical Questions*.

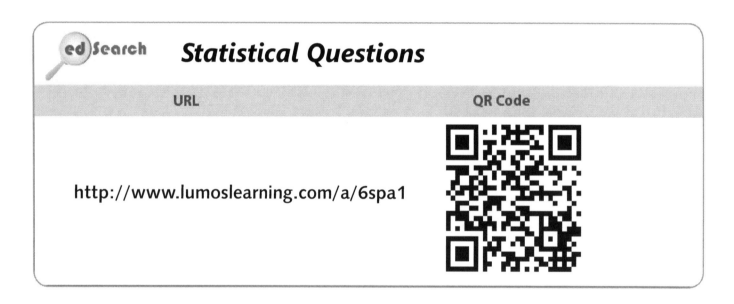

ed Search **Statistical Questions**

URL	QR Code
http://www.lumoslearning.com/a/6spa1	

1. The chart below shows the participation of a sixth grade class in its school's music activities. Each student was allowed to pick one music activity.

   How many boys are in the sixth grade?

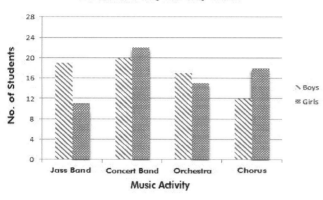

   Ⓐ 86
   Ⓑ 68
   Ⓒ 42
   Ⓓ 12

2. A student wanted to know what the sixth grade girls' favorite song was. What would be the best way to conduct a survey?

   Ⓐ Do an Internet search of favorite songs of young girls.
   Ⓑ Survey the sixth grade boys.
   Ⓒ Survey the sixth grade girls.
   Ⓓ Conduct a survey at the mall.

3. Emily wanted to know what the range of daily temperatures this past week was. What would be the best way of conducting her survey?

   Ⓐ Take the temperature once during the week.
   Ⓑ Take the temperature only in the morning.
   Ⓒ Take the temperature only in the evening.
   Ⓓ Take the temperature two times a day, at the warmest and coolest times of the day.

4. **Goldie wants to find out how many presents children get for their birthdays. She surveys 11 families in the same neighborhood to find out how many presents their children get. Did Goldie get a representative sample?**

   Ⓐ No because she did not ask the right questions.
   Ⓑ No because she asked families in the same neighborhood who most likely have similar income levels.
   Ⓒ Yes because she asked families in the same neighborhood who most likely have similar income levels.
   Ⓓ Yes because she asked the right questions.

5. **Roberta is an arborist. She is studying maple trees in a specific area. Roberta wants to show a class the difference in the heights of the trees so that they can compare them. What type of graph would be best for that?**

   Ⓐ Line graph
   Ⓑ Picture graph
   Ⓒ Circle graph
   Ⓓ Bar graph

6. **Derek spends an average of 37 minutes a weekday on homework. He wants to know how much time other students in fourth grade spend on homework so he asks only students in his class. Will Derek's survey be biased?**

   Ⓐ Yes because he is asking fourth graders.
   Ⓑ No because he is asking fourth graders.
   Ⓒ Yes because students in his class have the same amount of homework as he does.
   Ⓓ No because students in his class have the same amount of homework as he does.

7. **There are five cities in New York State who compete for the title of "The Snowiest City." A survey is done to find the average snowfall. The average snowfall of all 5 cities is 112.6 inches. Cities 1 and 2 both get 116 inches of snow. City 3 gets 110.4 inches of snow. City 4 gets 119.6 inches of snow. City 5 gets 101 inches of snow. Which graph would best represent this information?**

   Ⓐ Picture graph
   Ⓑ Circle graph
   Ⓒ Bar graph
   Ⓓ Line graph

8. **Brooke is doing a survey to find out what percentage of time families spend together doing activities. She collects all of the data about the time spent together doing those different activities and wants to put it into a graph. Which graph would be best?**

Ⓐ Circle graph
Ⓑ Picture graph
Ⓒ Line graph
Ⓓ Bar graph

9. **Peter and Paul are playing cards. They each randomly select 12 cards to start the game. Are the cards that they each selected a biased sample?**

Ⓐ No because they were randomly selected.
Ⓑ Yes because they were randomly selected.
Ⓒ Yes because they are not at least 10% of the deck.
Ⓓ No because they are not at least 10% of the deck.

10. **Cara likes to go running. She runs 4 days a week. On Monday, she runs 7 miles. On Wednesday, she runs 3.4 miles. On Friday, she runs 5 miles. On Saturday she runs 7.4 miles. Cara wants to put her data into a graph so that she can visually see the fluctuation in the miles she runs. What graph would be best?**

Ⓐ Circle graph
Ⓑ Bar graph
Ⓒ Line graph
Ⓓ Picture graph

11. **Select the questions that qualify as statistical questions. Choose all that apply.**

Ⓐ How many letters are in my last name?
Ⓑ How many letters are in the last names of the students in my 6th grade class?
Ⓒ What are the colors of the shoes worn by the students in my school?
Ⓓ What are the heart rates of the students in a 6th grade class?
Ⓔ How many hours of sleep per night do 6th graders usually get when they have school the next day?

12. Match the correct data plot for each question. Write the letters (in capitals) in the box.

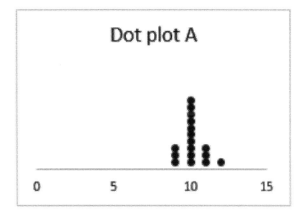

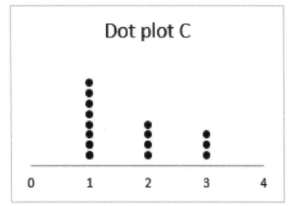

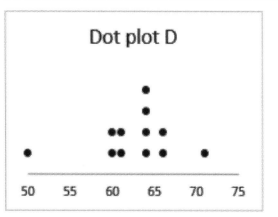

Question	Dot Plot ___
1. What are the ages of 4th graders in our school?	
2. What are the heights of the players on the 8th grade boys' basketball team?	
3. How many hours do 6th graders in our class watch TV on a school night?	
4. How many different languages do students in our class speak?	

Chapter 6

Lesson 2: Distribution

You can scan the QR code given below or use the url to access additional EdSearch resources including videos and mobile apps related to *Distribution*.

ed)Search   **Distribution**

URL	QR Code
http://www.lumoslearning.com/a/6spa2	

1. **If the total sales for socks was $60, what is the best estimate for the total sales of pants?**

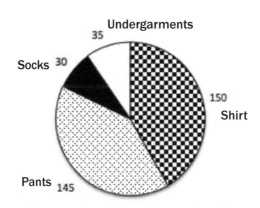

Ⓐ $200
Ⓑ $300
Ⓒ $60
Ⓓ $1,000

Note: Data represent the angles for each category

2. **The sixth graders at Kilmer Middle School can choose to participate in one of the four music activities offered. The number of students participating in each activity is shown in the bar graph below. Use the information shown to respond to the following: How many sixth graders are in the Jazz Band?**

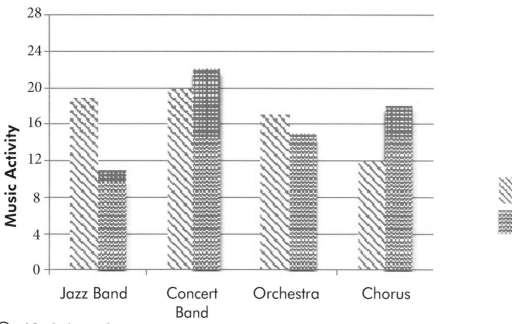

Ⓐ 19 sixth graders
Ⓑ 20 sixth graders
Ⓒ 30 sixth graders
Ⓓ 25 sixth graders

3. A .J. has downloaded 400 songs onto his computer. The songs are from a variety of genres. The circle graph below shows the breakdown (by genre) of his collection. Use the information shown to respond to the following: About how many more R + B songs than rock songs has A.J. downloaded?

A.J.'s Music Collections

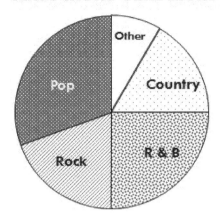

Ⓐ 20 more songs
Ⓑ 30 more songs
Ⓒ 50 more songs
Ⓓ 75 more songs

4. Colleen has to travel for work. In one week, she traveled all five work days. The shortest distance she traveled was 63 miles. The range of miles that she traveled was 98 miles. What is the longest distance that Colleen traveled for work in one week?

Ⓐ 161 miles
Ⓑ 98 miles
Ⓒ 33 miles
Ⓓ It cannot be determined.

5. Bob is a mailman. He delivers a lot of letters every day. His mail bag will only hold so many letters. The most letters that Bob has ever delivered in a day is 8,476. The range of the number of letters that Bob has ever delivered is 6,930. What is the least number of letters that Bob has ever delivered in one day?

Ⓐ 15,406 letters
Ⓑ 1,546 letters
Ⓒ 1,556 letters
Ⓓ It cannot be determined.

6. Fred goes with Katie to the art sale to try to find a gift for his mother. There are 66 pieces of art for sale. The median price is $280. Fred has $280 to spend. What is the minimum number of art pieces Fred can choose from?

    Ⓐ 16
    Ⓑ 33
    Ⓒ 65
    Ⓓ 22

7. Joann loves to watch the birds outside of her window. There is a robin that comes back every year to build a nest and lay her eggs. Joann keeps track of how many eggs the robin lays. The first year Joann keeps track, the robin lays 9 eggs and that is the least number of eggs she lays. The range of eggs that the robin has laid is one third the number of eggs from the first year. What are the most eggs the robin has ever laid?

    Ⓐ 21 eggs
    Ⓑ 12 eggs
    Ⓒ 14 eggs
    Ⓓ 27 eggs

8. Matt loves to watch movies. He has a movie collection that has 285 movies in it. The length of time of all of his movies range from 48 minutes to 3 hours and 26 minutes. What is the range of the length of time of Matt's movies?

    Ⓐ 3 hours and 38 minutes
    Ⓑ 1 hour and 58 minutes
    Ⓒ 2 hours and 58 minutes
    Ⓓ 2 hours and 38 minutes

9. Jessica is a photographer. She is putting together photo albums to show off her photographs. The first photo album has 50 pictures in it. The second photo album has 119 pictures in it. The third photo album has 174 pictures in it. The fourth photo album has 72 pictures in it. The fifth photo album has 61 pictures in it. What is the range?

    Ⓐ 102
    Ⓑ 174
    Ⓒ 124
    Ⓓ 113

10. Sam is a shrimp fisherman. In one month, Sam gets a maximum of 280 pounds of shrimp. The minimum that Sam gets is half of his maximum. What is the range in the pounds of shrimp that Sam gets?

    Ⓐ 120
    Ⓑ 280
    Ⓒ 100
    Ⓓ 140

11. Wrapping paper rolls are sold in packages of 2, 4, or 6. The following prices apply to the packages:

Package of 2 rolls —— $1.50
Package of 4 rolls —— $2.50
Package of 6 rolls —— $3.50

Lisa needs to buy exactly 12 rolls of wrapping paper for a service project.
Below are a few of the possible combinations. Select the value that correctly represents the missing number in the combinations listed on the table.

	2	4	6
2, 2, 2, 2, 2, **a** or 6 ($1.50) = $9.00: a =	○	○	○
2, 2, 2, **b**, 4 or 4($1.50)) + $2.50 = $8.50: b =	○	○	○
2, 2, **c**, 4, or 2($1.50) + 2($2.50) = $8.00: c =	○	○	○

12. The height of the four tallest downtown buildings of three different cities is given in the table below. Calculate the mean height of each city's buildings and match it with the correct answer from the bottom table.

City A Buildings	Height (m)
1	23
2	32
3	35
4	45

City B Buildings	Height (m)
1	15
2	22
3	28
4	25

City C Buildings	Height (m)
1	15
2	30
3	35
4	36

	22.50 m	29 m	23.20 m	33.75 m	18 m
City A Buildings	○	○	○	○	○
City B Buildings	○	○	○	○	○
City C Buildings	○	○	○	○	○

Chapter 6

Lesson 3: Central Tendency

You can scan the QR code given below or use the url to access additional EdSearch resources including videos and mobile apps related to *Central Tendency*.

ed)Search	Central Tendency	
URL		**QR Code**
http://www.lumoslearning.com/a/6spa3		

1 Jason was conducting a scientific experiment using bean plants. He measured the height (in centimeters) of each plant after three weeks. These were his measurements (in cm): 12, 15, 11, 17, 19, 21, 13, 11, 16

What is the average (mean) height? What is the median height?

Ⓐ Mean = 15 cm, Median = 19 cm
Ⓑ Mean = 15 cm, Median = 15 cm
Ⓒ Mean = 19 cm, Median = 15 cm
Ⓓ Mean = 15 cm, Median = 13 cm

2. Stacy has 60 pairs of shoes. She has shoes that have a heel height of between 1 inch and 4 inches. Stacy has 20 pairs of shoes that have a 1 inch heel, 15 pairs of shoes that have a 2 inch heel and 20 pairs of shoes that have a 3 inch heel height. Remaining shoes have 4 inch heel height. What is the average heel height of all 60 pairs of Stacy's shoes?

Ⓐ 1.3 inches
Ⓑ 1.5 inches
Ⓒ 2 inches
Ⓓ 2.2 inches

3. What is the median of the following set of numbers?
{16, −10, 13, −8, −1, 5, 7, 10}
Ⓐ −8
Ⓑ −1
Ⓒ 4
Ⓓ 6

4. Given the following set of data, is the median or the mode larger?
{5, −10, 14, 6, 8, −2, 11, 3, 6}
Ⓐ The mode
Ⓑ The median
Ⓒ They are the same
Ⓓ You cannot figure it out

5. A = { 10, 15, 2, 14, 19, 25, 0 }

Which of the following numbers, if added to Set A, would have the greatest effect on its median?
Ⓐ 14
Ⓑ 50
Ⓒ 5
Ⓓ 15

6. **What is the mean, median and mode for the following data?**

   {−7, 18, 29, 4, −3, 11, 22}

   Ⓐ Mean = 10
     Median = 18
     Mode = −3

   Ⓑ Mean = 11
     Median = 11
     Mode = none

   Ⓒ Mean = 10.57
     Median = 11
     Mode = none

   Ⓓ Mean = 10
     Median = 18
     Mode = −3

7. **Amanda had the following numbers: 1,2,6**

   If she added the number 3 to the list...

   Ⓐ the mean would increase
   Ⓑ the mean would decrease
   Ⓒ the median would increase
   Ⓓ the median would decrease

8. **A pizza shop sells the following ice cream treats:**

   Strawberry Gelato: $0.60
   Chocolate Cone: $0.80
   Lemon Ice: $0.45

   What is the average sale price for the ice cream treats?

   Ⓐ $0.62
   Ⓑ $0.45
   Ⓒ $0.60
   Ⓓ $0.80

9. Marcel has 5 stamp collections. He wants to average 35 stamps per collection. So far, he has 28, 62, 12, and 44 stamps in each collection. How many stamps does he need to have in his 5th collection to average 35 stamps?

    Ⓐ 30
    Ⓑ 29
    Ⓒ 28
    Ⓓ 27

10. How much will the mean of the following set of numbers increase if the number 53 is added to it?
    {67, 29, 40, –12, 88, –7, 11}

    Ⓐ 53
    Ⓑ 2.768
    Ⓒ 2.571
    Ⓓ 6.625

11. Find the mean of the following set.
    { 25.1, 19.6, 88.5, 0, -3, 19.8 }
    Circle the correct answer.

    Ⓐ 19.6
    Ⓑ 26
    Ⓒ 25
    Ⓓ 19.7

12. Select the median number for each set of numbers.

	3	4	8
4, 2, 3, 6, 4, 9, 7	○	○	○
6, 3, 2, 8, 1, 3, 6	○	○	○
8, 9, 4, 8, 1, 10, 3	○	○	○

13. Select the median number for each set of numbers.

	11	15	18
12, 18, 11, 20, 20	○	○	○
14, 20, 18, 11, 15	○	○	○
8, 6, 15, 11, 18	○	○	○

Chapter 6

Lesson 4: Graphs & Charts

You can scan the QR code given below or use the url to access additional EdSearch resources including videos and mobile apps related to *Graphs & Charts*.

URL	QR Code
http://www.lumoslearning.com/a/6spb4	

1. **Which of the following graphs best represents the values in this table?**

X	Y
1	1
2	3
3	1
4	3

Ⓐ
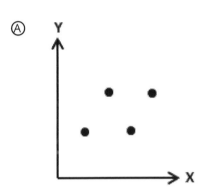

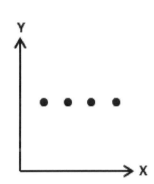

Ⓑ
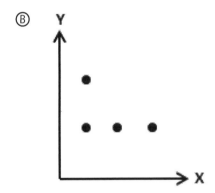

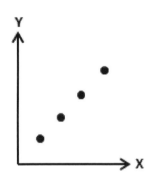

2. The results of the class' most recent science test are displayed in this histogram. Use the results to answer the question. A "passing" score is 61 or higher.

How many students passed the science test?

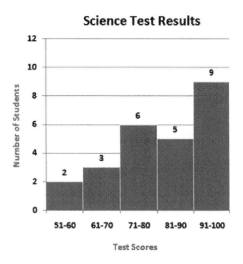

Ⓐ 3 students
Ⓑ 20 students
Ⓒ 23 students
Ⓓ 25 students

3. The results of the class' most recent science test are displayed in this histogram. Use the results to answer the question. How many students scored a 90 or below?

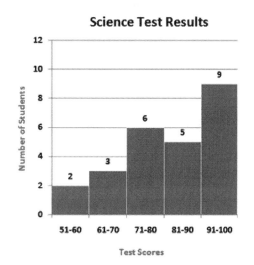

Ⓐ 5 students
Ⓑ 9 students
Ⓒ 11 students
Ⓓ 16 students

4. As part of their weather unit, the students in Mr. Green's class prepared a line graph showing the high and low temperatures recorded each day during a one-week period. Use the graph to answer the question.

On which day was the greatest range in temperature seen?

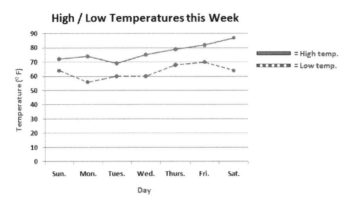

Ⓐ Sunday
Ⓑ Monday
Ⓒ Friday
Ⓓ Saturday

5. The sixth graders at Kilmer Middle School can choose to participate in one of the four music activities offered. The number of students participating in each activity is shown in the bar graph below. Use the information shown to answer the question.

There are 180 sixth graders in the school. About how many do not participate in one of the music activities?

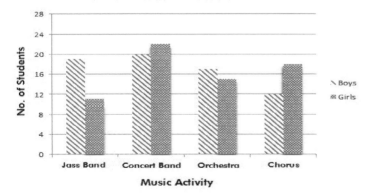

Ⓐ 66 students
Ⓑ 46 students
Ⓒ 25 students
Ⓓ 15 students

6. A.J. has downloaded 400 songs onto his computer. The songs are from a variety of genres. The circle graph below shows the breakdown of his collection by genre. Use the information shown to answer the question.

    Which two genres together make up more than half of A.J.'s collection?

    A.J.'s Music Collections

    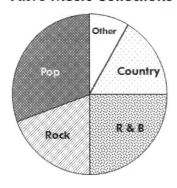

    Ⓐ R + B and Country
    Ⓑ Country and Rock
    Ⓒ Rock and Pop
    Ⓓ Pop and R + B

7. The results of the class' most recent science test are displayed in this histogram. Use the results to answer the question.

    What percentage of the class scored an 81-90 on the test?

    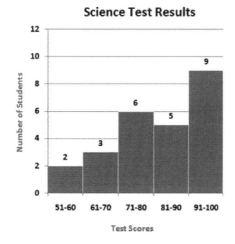

    Ⓐ 5%
    Ⓑ 20%
    Ⓒ 25%
    Ⓓ 30%

8. How much of the graph do undergarments and socks make up together?

Clothing Sales Breakdown

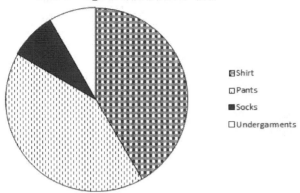

☒ Shirt
☐ Pants
■ Socks
☐ Undergarments

(A) less than 5%
(B) between 5% and 10%
(C) between 10% and 25%
(D) more than 25%

9. As part of their weather unit, the students in Mr. Green's class prepared a line graph showing the high and low temperatures recorded each day during a one-week period. Use the graph to answer the question.

What percentage of the days had a high temperature of 80 degrees or higher? Round to the nearest tenth.

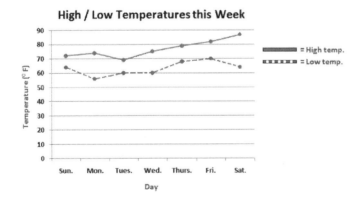

(A) 14.3%
(B) 42.9%
(C) 28.6%
(D) None of these

10. **The sixth graders at Kilmer Middle School can choose to participate in one of the four music activities offered. The number of students participating in each activity is shown in the bar graph below. Use the information shown to answer the question.**

There are 132 students who participate in music activities. What percentage of students who participate in music activities participate in chorus or jazz band?

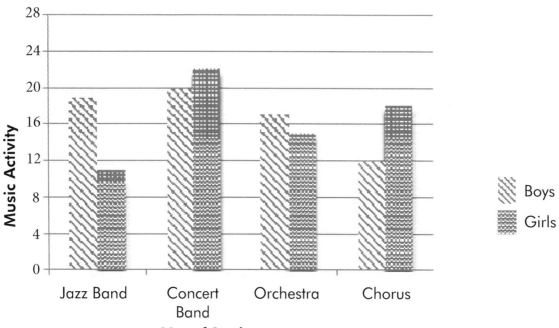

Ⓐ 45%
Ⓑ 38%
Ⓒ 40%
Ⓓ 50%

Refer below bar graph to answer the following questions.

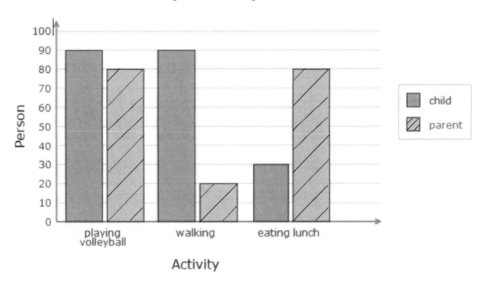

11. **Which of the following statements are true? Select all that apply.**

    Ⓐ The same number of children participated in playing volleyball and walking

    Ⓑ The same number of children participated in walking and eating lunch.

    Ⓒ All of the children who played volleyball also ate lunch.

    Ⓓ More children than parents ate lunch.

    Ⓔ More children than parents played volleyball.

    Ⓕ The same number of parents played volleyball as ate lunch.

12. **What is the total number of parents and children who played volleyball and ate lunch? Write your answer in the box below.**

Chapter 6

Lesson 5: Data Interpretation

You can scan the QR code given below or use the url to access additional EdSearch resources including videos and mobile apps related to *Data Interpretation*.

ed Search	**Data Interpretation**	
URL		**QR Code**
http://www.lumoslearning.com/a/6spb5		

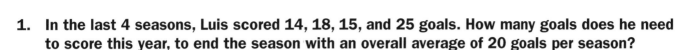

1. In the last 4 seasons, Luis scored 14, 18, 15, and 25 goals. How many goals does he need to score this year, to end the season with an overall average of 20 goals per season?

Ⓐ 29
Ⓑ 27
Ⓒ 30
Ⓓ 28

2. Stacy has 60 pairs of shoes. She has shoes that have a heel height of between 1 inch and 4 inches. Stacy wants to know which heel height she has the most of. Would she figure out the mode or mean?

Ⓐ Mean
Ⓑ Mode
Ⓒ Both
Ⓓ Neither

3. There are three ice cream stands within 15 miles and they are owned by Mr. Sno.

Ice Cream Stand	Vanilla	Chocolate	Twist
A	15	22	10
B	24	8	14
C	20	16	13

What percentage of the ice cream cones sold by Ice Cream Stand B were vanilla? Round your answer to the nearest whole number.

Ⓐ 52%
Ⓑ 24%
Ⓒ 50%
Ⓓ 25%

4. There are three ice cream stands within 15 miles and they are owned by Mr. Sno.

Ice Cream Stand	Vanilla	Chocolate	Twist
A	15	22	10
B	24	8	14
C	20	16	13

What percentage of the ice cream cones sold by Ice Cream Stand C were chocolate? Round your answer to the nearest whole number.

Ⓐ 30%
Ⓑ 32%
Ⓒ 33%
Ⓓ 62%

5. **Alexander plays baseball. His batting averages for the games he played this year were recorded. What is the batting average he had the most often?**

{.228, .316, .225, .333, .228, .125, .750, .500}

Ⓐ .228
Ⓑ .316
Ⓒ .750
Ⓓ .333

6. **How much will the mean increase by when the number 17 is added to the set? Round your numbers to the nearest tenth.**

{5, -10, 14, 6, 8, -2, 11, 3, 6}

Ⓐ 1.5
Ⓑ 1
Ⓒ 1.2
Ⓓ 1.7

7. **Andrea plays the violin. She is practicing songs for her concert and she times how long it takes her to play each song. She wants to put the song with the middle number of minutes at the beginning of her concert. How many minutes is the song that she will play first?**

{13, 8, 4, 16, 3, 9, 11}

Ⓐ 13 minutes
Ⓑ 11 minutes
Ⓒ 8 minutes
Ⓓ 9 minutes

8. **There are three ice cream stands within 15 miles and they are owned by Mr. Sno.**

Ice Cream Stand	Vanilla	Chocolate	Twist
A	15	22	10
B	20	8	14
C	24	16	13

What percentage of the total ice cream cones sold were twist? Round your answer to the nearest whole number.

Ⓐ 26%
Ⓑ 24%
Ⓒ 62%
Ⓓ 14%

9. Amy is trying to find out the number of magazines that have a woman on the cover. She goes to the book store and looks at the rack of magazines. There are at least 30 magazines. Amy looks at the covers of 20 magazines. Did Amy get a good sample?

Ⓐ Yes, because she looked at all of the magazines.
Ⓑ Yes, because she got a sample of more than half of the magazines.
Ⓒ No, because she did not looked at all of the covers.
Ⓓ No, because she looked at less than half of the magazines.

10. Travis is putting together outfits for work. He has 4 red shirts, 8 blue shirts and 7 white shirts. He has 6 pairs of khaki pants. What percent of Travis' possible outfits have blue shirts? Round your answer to the nearest whole number.

Ⓐ 8%
Ⓑ 43%
Ⓒ 42%
Ⓓ 48%

11. Travis is putting together outfits for work. He has 4 red shirts, 8 blue shirts and 7 white shirts. He has 6 pairs of khaki pants. What percent of Travis' possible outfits do not have red shirts?

12. Scientists were concerned about the survival of the Mississippi Blue Catfish, so they collected data from samples of this species of fish. The scientists captured the fish, measured them, and then returned them to the lake from which they were taken. Select the correct numbers for different ranges of lengths.

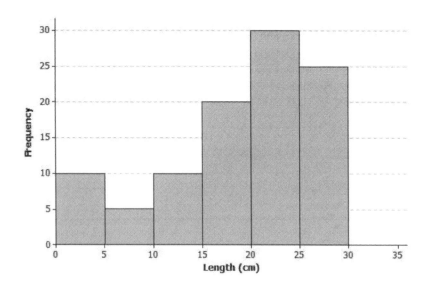

	5	10	20	25	30
0 – <5 cm	○	○	○	○	○
5 – <10 cm	○	○	○	○	○
10 – <15 cm	○	○	○	○	○
15 – <20 cm	○	○	○	○	○
20 – <25 cm	○	○	○	○	○

13. Each statement below describes a sample of data. Select all the statements that describe the situations that would result in non-biased or equal representation of the data.

Ⓐ Bella randomly called 100 phone numbers in her town to survey them about their shopping habits. 20 people chose to participate.

Ⓑ Heather climbed 11 trees throughout each forest in her county. Each forest is the same size.

Ⓒ Arujun bought 2 eggs from each farmer at the farmer's market. Each farmer had an equal number of eggs.

Ⓓ Allen put the names of all the cities in a state into a jar. Then he drew out 32 names from the jar.

Ⓔ Kiera polled 12 people at the town senior center.

Chapter 6

Lesson 6: Describing the Nature

You can scan the QR code given below or use the url to access additional EdSearch resources including videos and mobile apps related to *Describing the Nature*.

1. A new sandwich shop just opened. It is offering a choice of ham sandwiches, chicken sandwiches, or hamburgers as the main course and French fries, potato salad, baked beans or coleslaw to go with them. How many different ways can a customer have a sandwich and one side order?

Ⓐ 6
Ⓑ 8
Ⓒ 10
Ⓓ 12

2. Karen has a set of numbers that she is working with {6, 14, 28, 44, 2, −6}. What will happen to the mean if she adds the number −8 to the set?

Ⓐ The mean will decrease.
Ⓑ The mean will increase.
Ⓒ The mean will stay the same.
Ⓓ It cannot be determined.

3. Susan goes to the store to buy supplies to make a cake. What is the average amount that Susan spent on each of the ingredients she bought?
{$4.89, $2.13, $1.10, $3.75, $0.98, $2.46}

Ⓐ $5.22
Ⓑ $2.55
Ⓒ $2.25
Ⓓ $2.50

4. Robert had an average of 87.0 on his nine math tests. His scores on the first eight tests were {92, 96, 83, 81, 94, 78, 93, 70}. What score did Robert receive on his last test?

Ⓐ 90
Ⓑ 89
Ⓒ 96
Ⓓ 87

5. Terry is playing a game with his brother and they played 5 times. The median score that Terry got was 37. The range of Terry's scores was 40. What was the lowest and highest score that Terry got?

Ⓐ 37 and 77
Ⓑ 10 and 50
Ⓒ 17 and 57
Ⓓ Not enough information is given.

6. **Marcus wants to find out how many people go to the zoo on Saturdays in August. The zoo is open for 7 hours and there are 4 Saturdays in August. He counts the number of people who enter the zoo for two hours one Saturday. Will Marcus get an accurate idea of how many people go to the zoo?**

   Ⓐ Yes because he will get a good representative sample.
   Ⓑ No because he will not get enough of a representative sample.
   Ⓒ Yes because he can assume that two hours is enough time to count the number of people.
   Ⓓ No because he would need to be there for less time.

7. **Carl surveys his class to find out how tall his classmates are.**
   How many classmates did Carl survey?

Height	Number of Classmates
4'4" – 4'8"	1
4'9" – 5'	4
5'1" – 5'5"	7
5'6" – 5'11"	14
6' – 6'4"	2

   Ⓐ 27
   Ⓑ 28
   Ⓒ 14
   Ⓓ 24

8. **Julie is making a quilt. She uses 7 different patterns for her quilt squares.**

   What percentage of Julie's quilt is not flowers or butterflies?

Squares	Number
Solid	15
Stripe	22
Flower	8
Plaid	12
Zig-Zag	13
Circles	10
Butterflies	6

   Ⓐ 80%
   Ⓑ 72%
   Ⓒ 84%
   Ⓓ 83%

9. Carl surveys his class to find out how tall his classmates are.

   How many classmates are taller than 5 feet?

Height	Number of Classmates
4'4" – 4'8"	1
4'9" – 5'	4
5'1" – 5'5"	7
5'6" – 5'11"	14
6' – 6'4"	2

Ⓐ 23
Ⓑ 14
Ⓒ 27
Ⓓ 16

10. Travis is putting together outfits for work. He has 4 red shirts, 8 blue shirts and 7 white shirts. He has 6 pairs of khaki pants. What percent of Travis' possible outfits do not have red shirts?

Ⓐ 79%
Ⓑ 90%
Ⓒ 78%
Ⓓ 15%

11. What is the mean of these numbers? 5, 4, 3, 7, 8, 9. Circle the correct answer choice.

Ⓐ 6
Ⓑ 5
Ⓒ 7
Ⓓ 3

12. Dana's recent math exams grades were: 67, 62, 70, 69, 90, 93, 95, 88, and 93. What is Dana's median score? Circle the answer that represents the median score.

Ⓐ 88
Ⓑ 93
Ⓒ 67

Chapter 6

Lesson 7: Context of Data Gathered

You can scan the QR code given below or use the url to access additional EdSearch resources including videos and mobile apps related to *Context of Data Gathered.*

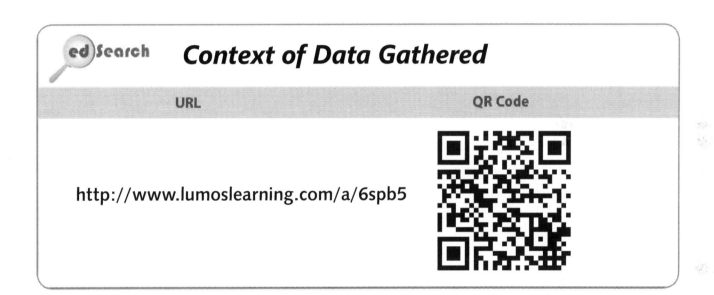

ed Search **Context of Data Gathered**

URL	QR Code
http://www.lumoslearning.com/a/6spb5	

1. **Bella recorded the number of newspapers left over at the end of each day for a week. What is the average number of newspapers left each day?**

   3, 6, 1, 0, 2, 3, 6

   Ⓐ 2 newspapers
   Ⓑ 3 newspapers
   Ⓒ 4.3 newspapers
   Ⓓ 6 newspapers

2. **Recorded below are the ages of eight friends. Which statement is true about this data set?**

   13, 18, 14, 12, 15, 19, 11, 15

   Ⓐ Mean > Median > Mode
   Ⓑ Mode < Mean < Median
   Ⓒ Median > Mode < Median
   Ⓓ Mode > Mean > Median

3. **The line plot below represents the high temperature in °F each day of a rafting trip. What was the average high temperature during the trip?**

   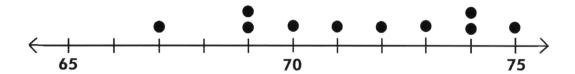

   Ⓐ 70°F
   Ⓑ 71°F
   Ⓒ 71.4°F
   Ⓓ 72°F

4. **What is the mean absolute deviation of the grades Charlene received on her first ten quizzes: 83%, 92%, 76%, 87%, 89%, 96%, 88%, 91%, 79%, 99%.**

   Ⓐ 4.5%
   Ⓑ 5.4%
   Ⓒ 88%
   Ⓓ 88.5%

5. The following numbers are the minutes it took Nyak to complete one lap around a certain dirt bike course. What is the mean absolute deviation of this data set?

12.3, 12.6, 12.2, 10.9, 11.3, 10.3, 11.7, 10.7

Ⓐ 0.7 minutes
Ⓑ 0.75 minutes
Ⓒ 11.1 minutes
Ⓓ 1.5 minutes

6. The local Akita Rescue Organization has nine Akitas for adoption. Their weights are 82 lbs, 95, lbs, 130 lbs, 112 lbs, 122 lbs, 72 lbs, 86, lbs, 145 lbs, 93 lbs. What are the median (M), 1st Quartile (Q1), 3rd Quartile (Q3) and Interquartile Range (IQR) of this data set?

Ⓐ M = 95, Q1 = 84, Q3 = 126, IQR = 42
Ⓑ M = 95, Q1 = 85, Q3 = 126, IQR = 145
Ⓒ M = 95, Q1 = 84, Q3 = 145, IQR = 42
Ⓓ M = 95, Q1 = 126, Q3 = 145, IQR = 42

7. Monica is keeping track of how much money she spends on lunch each school day. This week Monica spent $5.20, $6.50, $3.75, $0.75, and $4.15. What is the median (M) and Interquartile Range (IQR) of Monica's lunch expense?

Ⓐ M = $4.15, IQR = $1.45
Ⓑ M = $4.07, IQR = $1.45
Ⓒ M = $4.07, IQR = $2.25
Ⓓ M = $4.15, IQR = $3.60

8. Monica's friend Anna is also tracking her school lunch expenses. This week Anna spent $2.60, $0, $7.00, $4.40, $3.75. What is the difference between Monica's and Anna's average daily lunch expense?

Monica: $5.20, $6.50, $3.75, $0.75, and $4.15

Ⓐ $0.40
Ⓑ $0.52
Ⓒ $0.60
Ⓓ $1.50

9. **Zahra and Tyland are very competitive. Each have recorded their basketball scores since the beginning of the season. Which data set has a greater Interquartile Range (IQR)?**

Name	Scores
Zahra	8, 10, 3, 12, 14, 11
Tyland	6, 7, 18, 12, 4, 9

Ⓐ Zahra has the higher IQR of 4.
Ⓑ Zahra has the higher IQR of 10.5.
Ⓒ Tyland's IQR is 2 points higher than Zahra's.
Ⓓ Tyland and Zahra have the same IQR of 5.

10. **Jamila records the number of customers she gets each day for a week: 20, 42, 15, 23, 53, 62, 58. What is the mean absolute deviation of this data?**

Ⓐ 16.9 customers
Ⓑ 19 customers
Ⓒ 39 customers
Ⓓ 47.5 customers

11. **Frank played 9 basketball games this season. His scores were 15, 20, 14, 36, 20, 10, 35, 23, and 24. What is the median of Frank's scores? Write the answer in the box.**

12. **Gordan has the following data: 13, 19, 16, z, 17**
If the mean is 16, which number could be z? Circle the correct answer.

Ⓐ 11
Ⓑ 15
Ⓒ 18

Chapter 6

Lesson 8: Relating Data Distributions

You can scan the QR code given below or use the url to access additional EdSearch resources including videos and mobile apps related to *Relating Data Distributions*.

ed Search

Relating Data Distributions

URL	QR Code
http://www.lumoslearning.com/a/6spb5	

1. The histogram below shows the grades in Mr. Didonato's history class.

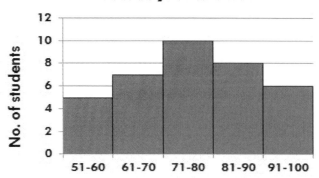

Which of the following statements is true based on this data?

Ⓐ The mode score is 75%.
Ⓑ More than half the students received 81% or higher.
Ⓒ Ten students received a 70% or lower.
Ⓓ There is not enough information to determine the median score.

2. The bar graph below shows the different types of shoes sold by *Active Feet.*

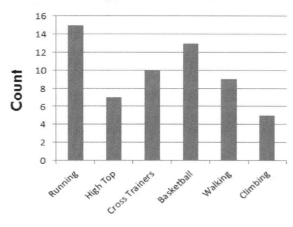

Which of the following statements is true based on this data?

Ⓐ The store carries more types of basketball and climbing shoes combined than types of running shoes.
Ⓑ The store sells more running shoes than any other shoe type.
Ⓒ The store has more types of walking shoes than cross trainers.
Ⓓ The store earns more money selling basketball shoes than walking shoes.

3. Milo and Jacque went fishing and recorded the weight of their fish in the line plots below.

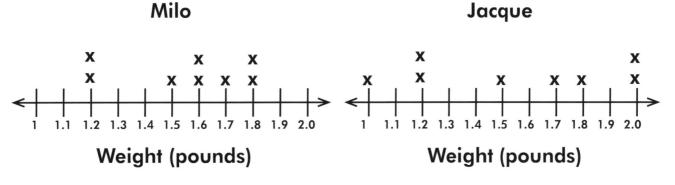

Which of the following statements is true based on this data?

Ⓐ The weights of Milo's fish have more variability.
Ⓑ The average weight of Jacque's fish is greater than the average weight of Milo's fish.
Ⓒ The weights of Jacque's fish have a greater mean absolute deviation.
Ⓓ Milo caught more fish by weight than Jacque.

4. The frequency table below records the age of the student who attended the dance.

Age	Frequency
11	17
12	20
13	9
14	8
15	12
16	4

Which of the following statements is true based on this data?
Ⓐ 80 students attended the dance.
Ⓑ The mean age is 12.86
Ⓒ If 3 more 16-year-olds arrive, the median age would increase.
Ⓓ More than half the students are older than the mean.

5. For twelve weeks Jeb has recorded his car's fuel mileage in miles per gallon (mpg). He has plotted these fuel mileages below in a box plot.

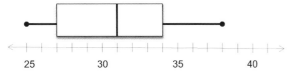

Which of the following statements is true based on this data?

Ⓐ The best fuel mileage recorded was 34 mpg.
Ⓑ Half of the data collected was between 27 mpg and 34 mpg.
Ⓒ The median fuel mileage was 30.5 mpg.
Ⓓ Three data points lie in the Interquartile range.

6. *"Forever Green"* recorded the heights of the pine trees sold this month in the box plot shown below. **There are 15 data points in Quartile 3.**

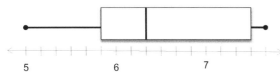

Which of the following statements is true based on this data?

Ⓐ About 25% of the trees were 7 feet 3 inches or taller.
Ⓑ There are more data points in Quartile 2 than Quartile 3.
Ⓒ The median height is 6 feet 2 inches.
Ⓓ "Forever Green" sold a total of about 60 trees this month.

7. As part of a math project, each student in Ms. Lauzon's class recorded the number of jumping jacks they could perform in 30 seconds.

Stem	Leaf
3	0 0 2 4 7 7
4	1 1 4 7 9
5	2 3 4 4 6 6 7
6	0 0 1 1 3 8 8
7	1 2
3|0 means 30	

Which of the following statements is true based on this data?

Ⓐ There are 21 students in Ms. Lauzon's class.
Ⓑ The median number of jumping jacks performed was 53.
Ⓒ The range of jumping jacks is 42.
Ⓓ Seven people performed less than 40 jumping jacks.

8. **Tamryn and Clio both make beaded necklaces. The line plots below display the number of beads on ten necklaces each from Tamryn and Clio.**

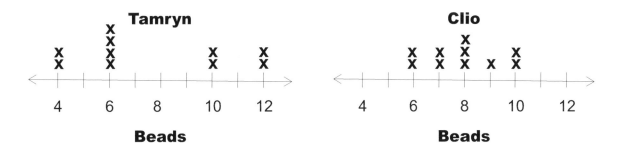

Which of the following statements is true based on this data?

Ⓐ If Tamryn added an eleventh data point of 10, the mean would not change.
Ⓑ On an average, Tamryn uses more beads than Clio.
Ⓒ Clio has more variability in the number of beads she uses.
Ⓓ If Clio added an eleventh data point of 8, the median would stay the same.

9. **The histogram below shows the high temperature each day for a month.**

Temperature, Fahrenheit

Which of the following statements is true based on this data?

Ⓐ More than half the days had a temperature of 70–74°.
Ⓑ 20% of the days had temperatures above 74°.
Ⓒ The average temperature was 72°.
Ⓓ There were fewer days below 70° than days above 74°.

10. Marcel enjoys catching fireflies. The steam-and-leaf plot shows the number of fireflies Marcel caught on several nights.

Stem	Leaf
0	4 6 9
1	0 3 4 7 7 7 8
2	0 0 2 2 5
3	1 4
1|3 means 13	

Which of the following statements is true based on this data?

Ⓐ The median is greater than the mean.
Ⓑ The median number of fireflies caught was 17.
Ⓒ The range of fireflies is 34.
Ⓓ Marcel caught fireflies on 14 nights.

11. The students in one math class were asked how many brothers and sisters (siblings) they each have. The plot below shows the distribution of the data (answers from the students). Circle the blue box that represents the number of siblings had by the most students in this class.

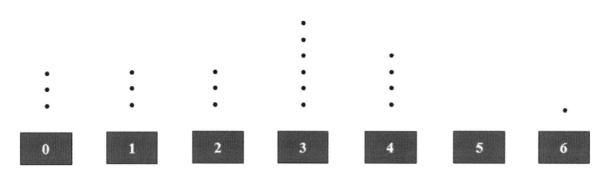

12. Three volleyball teams each recorded their scores for their first 5 games. Use each team's scores below to determine the missing value.

	10	14	17
Team 1: 15, 16, t, 17, 12, Mode = 17, What is t?	○	○	○
Team 2: 7, 14, r, 16, 13 Mean = 12, What is r?	○	○	○
Team 3: 11, 7, 19, 14, z, Median = 14, What is z?	○	○	○

End of Statistics & Probability

Chapter 6: Statistics & Probability

Answer Key
&
Detailed Explanations

Lesson 1: Statistical Questions

Question No.	Answer	Detailed Explanation
1	B	Add the number of boys who participated in each activity to find the total number of boys. $19 + 20 + 17 + 12 = 68$
2	C	When conducting a survey, it is most accurate to ask the question to the focus group you are trying to reach.
3	D	Taking the temperature consistently at the warmest and coolest time of the day will provide a consistent data sample for Emily's survey.
4	B	A representative sample should be a sample of people who represent the larger population. Surveying all families in one neighborhood would not be representative because people in the same neighborhood most likely have the same income level.
5	D	A bar graph would be best because it shows the data in bars that are then very easy to compare.
6	C	Derek's survey will be biased because the students in his class have the same amount of homework as he does. To get an unbiased sample, he should ask students from all fourth grade classes.
7	C	A bar graph will show the average snowfall of each city in a bar of different colors. Those bars will be very easy to compare and will make it easy to compare the average snowfall.
8	A	A circle graph is the best graph to use when representing percentages. The circle graph would show what percentage of a family's entire day is spent doing each activity.
9	A	The randomly selected cards are not biased. A biased sample is one that contains the same or very similar items. Randomly selected samples are generally not biased.
10	C	A line graph would be best because Cara can plot the miles she runs and connect them with line segments. She will then be able to visually see the fluctuation in the miles (the trend) in the distance she runs.
11	B, C, D & E	Options (B), (C), (D), and (E) are correct, A statistical question is one that can be answered by collecting data that vary (i.e., not all of the data values are the same).

Question No.	Answer	Detailed Explanation

12

Question	Dot Plot ___
1. What are the ages of 4th graders in our school?	**A**
2. What are the heights of the players on the 8th grade boys' basketball team?	**D**
3. How many hours do 6th graders in our class watch TV on a school night?	**C**
4. How many different languages do students in our class speak?	**B**

1. On the average, ages of 4th graders vary between 9 to 12 (most of them are 10 years old). Therefore, we can say that Dot Plot A represents the ages of 4th graders.

2. Heights of the students have more variations. Therefore, we can say that Dot Plot D represents the heights of 8th grade boys' basketball team (and note also that in Dot Plot D, there are 12 points, which correspond to 12 players in a basketball team).

3. Number of hours 6th graders watch TV may vary between 1 to 3 hour, which is represented in Dot Plot C.

4. In a class, there may be students who speak different languages, which may vary from 1 to 6, which is represented in Dot Plot B.

(In all the Dot plots, note also how range of x- values are different for different quantities such as age, number of languages, hour, and height.)

Lesson 2: Distribution

Question No.	Answer	Detailed Explanation
1	B	The Socks section has a measure of 30 degrees and the Pants section has a measure of 145 degrees. Solve for the total pant sales by setting up a proportion and solving. $\dfrac{145}{30} = \dfrac{x}{\$60}$ $(145)(\$60) = 30x$ $8700 = 30x$ $290 = x$ Therefore, 300 is the best estimate.
2	C	The graph shows that there are 19 boys and 11 girls participating in the Jazz Band. $19 + 11 = 30$ sixth graders altogether
3	A	Angle corresponding to R + B songs = 90 degrees. The number of R + B songs downloaded is $400 \times (\dfrac{90}{360}) = 400 \times (\dfrac{1}{4}) = 100$ songs $(\dfrac{90}{360} = \dfrac{1}{4}$ after taking GCF 90 out of both the numerator and denominator) Angle correspoding to rock songs is close to 90 degrees but less than 90 degrees. Let us take it to be 75 degrees (approximately) So, number of rock songs downloaded is $400 \times (\dfrac{75}{360}) = 400 \times (\dfrac{5}{24}) = 83$ (approximately) $(\dfrac{75}{360} = \dfrac{5}{24}$ after taking GCF 15 out of both the numerator and denominator) Therefore A.J. has downloaded $100 - 83 = 17$ more R + B songs than rock songs. Among the choices given, (A) is the most appropriate choice.
4	A	To find the longest distance Colleen traveled, add the shortest distance to the range. $63 + 98 = 161$
5	B	To find the least number of letters that Bob has ever delivered, subtract the range from the largest number. $8,476 - 6,930 = 1,546$ letters

Question No.	Answer	Detailed Explanation
6	B	The median price is $280 and there are 66 pieces of art for sale. That means that half of the pieces of art have a price of $280 or less. Fred has $280 to spend. That means that he has at least $\frac{1}{2}$ of the pieces of art to choose from. $\frac{66}{2} = 33$ There could be other art pieces priced at $280 above the median so that is why we say "at least".
7	B	To find the most number of eggs laid, add the least number of eggs to the range. The range is $\frac{1}{3}$ of 9 = 3. 9 + 3 = 12 eggs
8	D	The range is the difference between the largest and smallest numbers. To find the range, subtract 48 minutes from 3 hours and 26 minutes. Change 3 hours and 26 minutes to 206 minutes 206 − 48 = 158 minutes Two hours = 120 minutes Subtract 158 − 120 to get 38 minutes remaining That makes 2 hours and 38 minutes
9	C	The range is the difference between the smallest and largest number. The largest number is 174 and the smallest number is 50. Subtract 50 from 174 to find the range. 174 − 50 = 124
10	D	To find the range, subtract the smallest number from the largest number. The largest number is 280. The smallest number is half of 280. $\frac{280}{2} = 140$ 280 − 140 = 140
11		In the first combination, it is given that Lisa has already selected 2 x 5 = 10 paper rolls. Therefore, a = 12 - 10 = 2 In the second combination, it is given that Lisa has already selected (2 x 3) + (1 x 4) = 10 paper rolls. Therefore, b = 12 - 10 = 2 In the third combination, it is given that Lisa has already selected (2 x 2) + (1 x 4) = 8 paper rolls. Therefore, c = 12 - 8 = 4

Question No.	Answer	Detailed Explanation
12		City A = 33.75m City B = 22.50 m City C = 29 m Find the sum of the height of all four buildings and divide by 4 to determine the mean.

Question No.	Answer	Detailed Explanation

Lesson 3: Central Tendency

Question No.	Answer	Detailed Explanation
1	B	To find the average (mean) height of the plants, the heights would first be totaled. Then the total would be divided by 9 (the number of plants in all). 12 + 15 + 11 + 17 + 19 + 21 + 13 + 11 + 16 = 135. 135 divided by 9 equals 15. The average (mean) height is 15 centimeters. To find the median height, the numbers would be arranged in increasing order. The ordered set becomes: {11, 11, 12, 13, 15, 16, 17, 19, 21} The median is the middle value: 15 centimeters.
2	D	To find the average heel height, first figure out how many of each height Stacy has. Create an equation to figure out the number of 4 inch heels that Stacy has. Add 20 + 15 + 20 + x = 60 55 + x = 60 x = 5 Set up an equation to figure out the mean. You need to multiply the number of shoes and the heel height and then add them together and divide by the number of shoes. $$\frac{1(20) + 2(15) + 3(20) + 4(5)}{60} = x$$ x = 2.2 inches
3	D	To find the median, rearrange the numbers in the data set from lowest to highest. {16, −10, 13, −8, −1, 5, 7, 10} −10, −8, −1, 5, 7, 10, 13, 16 Because this set has an even number of terms, add the two middle numbers together and divide by 2. 5 + 7 = 12 12/2 = 6 6 is the median.
4	C	{5, −10, 14, 6, 8, −2, 11, 3, 6} The mode is 6 because it appears most often. To find the median, list the numbers in order from smallest to largest. −10, −2, 3, 5, 6, 6, 8, 11, 14 The median is 6 because it is in the middle.

Question No.	Answer	Detailed Explanation
5	C	0, 2, 10, 14, 15, 19, 25 Median is 14. (A) If 14 is added to the set, median = 14. So, it does not change. (B) If 50 is added to the set, median $= \dfrac{14+15}{2} = 14.5$. So, median increases by 0.5. (C) If 5 is added to the set, median $= \dfrac{10+14}{2} = 12$. So, median decreases by 2. (D) If 15 is added to the set, median $= \dfrac{14+15}{2} = 14.5$. So, median increases by 0.5. Therefore, median would be affected most by adding the score 5 to the set. Option (C) is the correct answer.
6	C	$\{-7, 18, 29, 4, -3, 11, 22\}$ There is no mode because no numbers repeat To find the median, list the numbers in order from smallest to largest. $-7, -3, 4, 11, 18, 22, 29$ The median $= 11$. To find the average, add all of the numbers together and divide by 7. $\dfrac{-7 + 18 + 29 + 4 + (-3) + 11 + 22}{7} = x$ $x = 10.57$
7	C	Mean for original set: $1 + 2 + 6 = 9$ $\dfrac{9}{3} = 3$ Median for original set: 2 Mean after adding 3: $1 + 2 + 3 + 6 = 12$ $\dfrac{12}{4} = 3$ Median after adding 3: $2 + 3 = 5$ $\dfrac{5}{2} = 2.5$
8	A	To find the average, add all of the prices together. $\$0.60 + \$0.80 + \$0.45 = \$1.85$ Then, divide by the number of ice cream treats. $\dfrac{\$1.85}{3} = \$0.616$, or $\$0.62$

Question No.	Answer	Detailed Explanation
9	B	For Marcel to have an average of 35 stamps, he will need to have a total of 175 stamps (5*35). Set up an equation to determine how many stamps the 5th collection should have. Let x represent the 5th collection. $28 + 62 + 12 + 44 + x = 175$ $146 + x = 175$ Subtract 146 from both sides. $146 + x - 146 = 175 - 146$ $x = 29$ stamps
10	B	$\{67, 29, 40, -12, 88, -7, 11\}$ the mean is 30.857 $\{67, 29, 40, -12, 88, -7, 11, 53\}$ the mean is 33.625 $33.625 - 30.857 = 2.768$
11	C	First, add the numbers in the set. $25.1 + 19.6 + 88.5 + 0 + -3 + 19.8 = 150$ Then divide the total by the number of terms in the set. $\dfrac{150}{6} = 25$

Question 12

	3	4	8
4, 2, 3, 6, 4, 9, 7		●	
6, 3, 2, 8, 1, 3, 6	●		
8, 9, 4, 8, 1, 10, 3			●

To determine the median number, first, order the set of numbers from least to greatest. The median number will be the number in the center.

Question 13

	11	15	18
12, 18, 11, 20, 20			●
14, 20, 18, 11, 15		●	
8, 6, 15, 11, 18	●		

To determine the median number, first, order the set of numbers from least to greatest. The median number will be the number in the center.

Lesson 4: Graphs & Charts

Question No.	Answer	Detailed Explanation
1	A	Using the data to create ordered pairs (x, y), the first choice is the only graph that accurately represents the ordered pairs.
2	C	To find the number of students who passed, add the number of students who scored in the ranges of $61 - 70$ (3), $71 - 80$ (6), $81-90$ (5), and $91 -100$ (9). $3 + 6 + 5 + 9 = 23$ students
3	D	To find the number of students who scored a 90 or below, add the number of students who scored in the ranges of $51 - 60$ (2), $61 - 70$ (3), $71 - 80$ (6), $81-90$ (5). $2 + 3 + 6 + 5 = 16$ students
4	D	On Saturday, the greatest range was seen, with a high temperature of 88 and a low temperature of 62, making the range 26 degrees.
5	B	Add together all of the students and then subtract that number from the total number. Jazz: 30 students Concert Band: 42 students Orchestra: 32 students Chorus: 30 students $30 + 42 + 32 + 30 = 134$ $180 - 134 = 46$ students do not participate in any kind of music activity
6	D	Pop and R & B together would make up more than half of the pie chart, or above 50%.
7	B	5 students scored an 81-90 on the test out of 25 students. Convert this fraction into percentage. $\frac{5}{25} \times 100 = 20\%$
8	C	Socks and undergarments together appear to take up more than a tenth, but less than a quarter, of the pie chart. The percentage would be between 10% and 25%.

Question No.	Answer	Detailed Explanation
9	C	Friday and Saturday both had temperatures of 80 degrees or higher. That means that $\frac{2}{7}$ days were 80 degrees or more. Convert $\frac{2}{7}$ into percentage by multiplying $\frac{2}{7}$ with 100. $\frac{2}{7} \times 100 = 28.57\%$ Round to the nearest tenth making the percentage 28.6%
10	A	Jazz Band: 19 + 11 = 30 students Chorus: 12 + 18 = 30 students 60 students participate in either jazz band or chorus. To find the percentage, divide 60 by 132. $60 \div 132 \approx 0.45$ To change the decimal to a percent, move the decimal point to the right two places. 0.45 = 45%
11	A, E, & F	A. 90 children participated in volleyball and 90 children participated in walking. E. 90 children played volleyball and only 80 parents played volleyball. F. 80 parents played volleyball and 80 parents ate lunch.
12	280	Parents volleyball: 80 Children volleyball: 90 Parents lunch: 80 Children lunch: 30 Total 280

Question No.	Answer	Detailed Explanation

Lesson 5: Data Interpretation

Question No.	Answer	Detailed Explanation
1	D	To determine the number of goals he would need, Luis will need a total of 100 (20 * 5) goals. Set up an equation. Let x represent the goals needed for the 5th season: $14 + 15 + 18 + 21 + x = 100$ $72 + x = 100$ Subtract 72 from both sides. $72 + x - 72 = 100$ $x = 28$
2	B	Stacy would figure out the mode. The mode will tell her which heel height occurs most often when she lists them out.
3	A	To figure out the percentage, add together all of the ice cream cones sold by stand B. $24 + 8 + 14 = 46$ To find the percentage, divide 24 by 46 $24/46 = .522$ (when rounded to the nearest thousandth) To make the decimal into a percentage, move the decimal point to the right two places and round down. 52%
4	C	To figure out the percentage, add together all of the ice cream cones sold by stand C. $20 + 16 + 13 = 49$ To find the percentage, divide 16 by 49 $16/49 = .327$ (when rounded to the nearest thousandth) To make the decimal into a percentage, move the decimal point to the right two places and round up. 33%
5	A	The number that shows up most often is the mode. .228 is the mode.
6	C	To find the mean, add all of the numbers together and divide by 9. $5 + -10 + 14 + 6 + 8 + -2 + 11 + 3 + 6 = 41$ $41 \div 9 \approx 4.6$ (when rounded to the nearest tenth) $5 + -10 + 14 + 6 + 8 + -2 + 11 + 3 + 6 + 17 = 58$ $58 \div 10 = 5.8$ When 17 is added, the mean is 5.8 $5.8 - 4.6 = 1.2$

Question No.	Answer	Detailed Explanation
7	D	Andrea needs to know the median. To find it, list all of the numbers in order from smallest to largest. 3, 4, 8, 9, 11, 13, 16
8	A	To figure out the percentage, add together all of the ice cream cones sold. Stand C: 20 + 16 + 13 = 49 Stand B: 24 + 8 + 14 = 46 Stand A: 15 + 22 + 10 = 47 49 + 47 + 46 = 142 Twist cones: 10 + 14 + 13 = 37 To find the percentage, divide 37 by 142 37/142 = .261 (when rounded to the nearest thousandth) To make the decimal into a percentage, move the decimal point to the right two places and round down. 26%
9	B	In order to get a representative sample, the person who is conducting the survey needs to get a good sample of what they are surveying. Amy looked at 20 magazines, which is more than half (2/3 to be exact)
10	C	Travis has 114 possible outfits. To figure that out you multiply the number of shirts by the number of khaki pants. 19 * 6 = 114 To find the outfits with blue shirts, multiply 8 by 6 to get 48 To find the percentage, divide 48 by 114. 48/114 = 0.421 (when rounded to the nearest thousandth) To make the decimal into a percentage, move the decimal point to the right two places and round down. 42% Alternate Method : Shirts can be chosen in (4 + 8 + 7) = 19 ways. Blue shirt can be chosen in 8 ways. To find the percentage of outfits with blue shirts, divide 8 by 19 8/19 = 0.421 (when rounded to the nearest thousandth) or 42.1% or 42% (when rounded to the nearest whole number)

Question No.	Answer	Detailed Explanation
11		Travis has 114 possible outfits. To figure that out you multiply the number of shirts by the number of khaki pants. 19 * 6 = 114

To find the outfits without red shirt, add together the blue and white shirts (8 + 7), multiply 15 by 6 to get 90

To find the percentage, divide 90 by 114.

90/114 = .789 (when rounded to the nearest thousandth)

To make the decimal into a percentage, move the decimal point to the right two places and round up.

79%

Alternate Method : Shirts can be chosen in (4 + 8 + 7) = 19 ways. Blue shirt or white shirt (i.e. outfits without red shirt) can be chosen in (8 + 7) = 15 ways.

To find the percentage of outfits without red shirts, divide 15 by 19

15/19 = 0.789 (when rounded to the nearest thousandth) or 78.9% or 79% (when rounded to the nearest whole number)

12

	5	10	20	25	30
0 – <5 cm		◉			
5 – <10 cm	◉				
10 – <15 cm		◉			
15 – <20 cm			◉		
20 – <25 cm					◉

13   B, C, & D   B, C, and D would be non-biased.

A would not be a good representation because participants were voluntary, which means those who chose to participate would most likely have similar shopping habits.

E would be biased because it targets a specific age group.

Question No.	Answer	Detailed Explanation

Lesson 6: Describing the Nature

1	D	Use the counting principle to determine the number of combinations if there are 3 types of sandwiches and 4 types of sides for lunch by: 3 * 4 = 12 There are 12 options.
2	A	{6, 14, 28, 44, 2, −6} the mean is 14.6 {6, 14, 28, 44, 2, −6, −8} the mean is 11.4 The mean will decrease with the addition of the number −8.
3	B	To find the average, add all of the prices together and divide by the number of ingredients, which is 6. $$\frac{\$4.89 +\$2.13 +\$1.10 +\$3.75 +\$0.98 +\$2.46}{6} = \$2.55$$
4	C	To receive an average of 87.0 on the 9 tests, Robert accumulated a total of 783 points. He scored a total of 687 on the first 8 tests. That means his score on the last test was 783 − 687 = 96.
5	D	Just knowing the median and the range is not enough information to figure out the lowest and highest scores.
6	B	In order to get a representative sample, the person who is conducting the survey needs to get a good sample of what they are surveying. Marcus would need to spend more than 2 hours at the zoo to get a good sample. He should also go on more than one Saturday.
7	B	To figure out how many classmates Carl surveyed, add together all of the numbers in the "Number of Classmates" column. 1 + 4 + 7 + 14 + 2 = 28
8	C	To figure out the percentage, figure out the total number of quilt squares. 15 + 22 + 8 + 12 + 13 + 10 + 6 = 86 Figure out how many squares are not flowers or butterflies. 15 + 22 + 12 + 13 + 10 = 72 To find the percentage, divide the number of squares that are not flowers or butterflies (72) by the total number of squares (86). $$\frac{72}{86} = .837$$ To make the decimal into a percentage, move the decimal point to the right two places and round up. 84%

Question No.	Answer	Detailed Explanation
9	A	To find out how many classmates are taller than 5 feet, add together all of the classmates that are 5' 1" or taller. 7 + 14 + 2 = 23
10	A	Travis has 114 possible outfits. To figure this out multiply the number of shirts by the number of khaki pants. 19 * 6 = 114 To find the outfits without a red shirt, add together the blue and white shirts (8 + 7), multiply 15 by 6 to get 90 To find the percentage, divide 90 by 114. $$\frac{90}{114} = .789$$ To make the decimal into a percentage, move the decimal point to the right two places and round up. 79%
11	A	The numbers added together equal 36, and 36/6 = 6
12	A	Dana's median score is 88.

Lesson 7: Context of Data Gathered

Question No.	Answer	Detailed Explanation
1	B	Find the total number of newspapers leftover and divide by the number of days. $$\frac{3+6+1+0+2+3+6}{7} = \frac{21}{7} = 3 \text{ newspapers}$$
2	D	Find the mean, median, and mode of the data set and compare. Mean: $\frac{13 + 18 + 14 + 12 + 15 + 19 + 11 + 15}{8} = \frac{117}{8} = 14.625$ Median: 11, 12, 13, 14, 15, 15, 18, 19 → 14.5 Mode: 15 Mode > Mean > Median
3	C	Add the temperatures and divide by the number of temperatures. $$\frac{67 + 69 + 69 + 70 + 71 + 72 + 73 + 74 + 74 + 75}{10} = \frac{714}{10} = 71.4°F$$
4	B	First find the mean. $$\frac{83 + 92 + 76 + 87 + 89 + 96 + 88 + 91 + 79 + 99}{10} = \frac{880}{10} = 88\%$$ Now find the distance between each number and the average. $\|83-88\|=5$ $\|92-88\|=4$ $\|76-88\|=12$ $\|87-88\|=1$ $\|89-88\|=1$ $\|96-88\|=8$ $\|88-88\|=0$ $\|91-88\|=3$ $\|79-88\|=9$ $\|99-88\|=11$ Take the average of these differences $\frac{5 + 4 + 12 + 1 + 1 + 8 + 0 + 3 + 9 + 11}{10} = \frac{54}{10} = 5.4\%$

Question No.	Answer	Detailed Explanation
5	A	First find the mean. $$\frac{12.3 + 12.6 + 12.2 + 10.9 + 11.3 + 10.3 + 11.7 + 10.7}{8} = \frac{92}{8} = 11.5$$ Now find the distance between each number and the average. $$|12.3-11.5|=0.8$$ $$|12.6-11.5|=1.1$$ $$|12.2-11.5|=0.7$$ $$|10.9-11.5|=0.6$$ $$|11.3-11.5|=0.2$$ $$|10.3-11.5|=1.2$$ $$|11.7-11.5|=0.2$$ $$|10.7-11.5|=0.8$$ Take the average of these differences $$\frac{0.8 + 1.1 + 0.7 + 0.6 + 0.2 + 1.2 + 0.2 + 0.8}{8} = \frac{5.6}{8} = 0.7\,min$$
6	A	Put the numbers in order from least to greatest. 72 82 86 93 95 112 122 130 145 Median = 95 $Q1 = \frac{82 + 86}{2} = 84$ $Q3 = \frac{122 + 130}{2} = 126$ IQR = 126 − 84 = 42 M = 95, Q1 = 84, Q3 = 126, IQR = 42
7	D	Put the numbers in order from least to greatest. $0.75 $3.75 $4.15 $5.20 $6.50 Median = $4.15 $Q1 = \frac{0.75 + 3.75}{2} = \$2.25$ $Q3 = \frac{5.20 + 6.50}{2} = \$5.85$ IQR = 5.85 - 2.25 = $3.60 M = $4.15, IQR = $3.60
8	B	Find the average of both and then find the difference. Anna: $\frac{2.60 + 0 + 7.00 + 4.40 + 3.7}{5} = \frac{17.75}{5} = \$3.55$ Monica: $\frac{5.20 + 6.50 + 3.75 + 0.75 + 4.1}{5} = \frac{20.35}{5} = \$4.07$ Difference: $4.07 − $3.55 = $0.52

Question No.	Answer	Detailed Explanation
9	C	Zahra: 3 8 10 11 12 14 Median $= \frac{10 + 11}{2} = \frac{21}{2} = 10.5$ Q1 = 8 Q3 = 12 IQR = 12 − 8 = 4 Tyland: 4 6 7 9 12 18 Median $= \frac{7 + 9}{2} = \frac{16}{2} = 8$ Q1 = 6 Q3 = 12 IQR = 12 − 6 = 6 Tyland has the greater IQR of 6, which is 2 points higher than Zahra's.
10	A	First find the mean. $$\frac{20 + 42 + 15 + 23 + 53 + 62 + 58}{7} = \frac{273}{7} = 39$$ Now find the distance between each number and the average. $\|20-39\|=19$ $\|42-39\|=3$ $\|15-39\|=24$ $\|23-39\|=16$ $\|53-39\|=14$ $\|62-39\|=23$ $\|58-39\|=19$ Take the average of these differences $$\frac{19 + 3 + 24 + 16 + 14 + 23 + 19}{7} = \frac{118}{7} = 16.9 \; customers$$
11	20	To find the median score, order the numbers from least to greatest. 10, 14, 15, 20, 20, 23, 24, 35, 36 Then identify the number that is in the middle. In this list, 20 is in the middle of the list so the median is 20.
12	B	(13 + 19 + 16 + z + 17) / 5 = 16 (65 + z) / 5 = 16 Multiply both sides by 5, 65 + z = 16 x 5 = 80 Subtract 65 from both sides to isolate z z = 80 - 65 = 15

Lesson 8: Relating Data Distributions

Question No.	Answer	Detailed Explanation
1	D	False. There is not enough information to determine the mode score.
		False. There are 14 out of 36 students who received an 81% or higher. This is less than a half of the students.
		False. Twelve students received a 70% or lower.
		True. We know that the median score (the average of the 18th and 19th number) falls between 71% and 80% but we do not know the specific value.
2	A	A) True. The store carries 13 basketball and 5 climbing shoe types for a total of 18 types. This is greater than 15 types, the number of running shoe types.
		B) False. The graph does not give any information about how much is sold.
		C) False. The store has 9 types of walking shoes and 10 types of cross trainers and thus has more types of cross trainers than walking shoes.
		D) False. The graph does not give any information about how much is sold.
3	C	A) False. The weights of Milo's fish have less variability as shown by the closeness of his data points.
		B) False. The average weight of Milo's fish is $\frac{1.2 + 1.2 + 1.5 + 1.6 + 1.6 + 1.7 + 1.8 + 1.8}{8} = \frac{12.4}{8} = 1.55$ *pounds*. The average weight of Jacque's fish is $\frac{1+1.2+1.2+1.5+1.7+1.8+2+2}{8} = \frac{12.4}{8} = 1.55$ *pounds*. Hence the average weights are the same.
		C) True. Without any calculations, you can see that Jacque's fish have weights that are farther away from the mean of 1.55 lbs than Milo's fish weight data.
		D) False. Milo and Jacque caught the same weight in fish. See (B) above.

Question No.	Answer	Detailed Explanation
4	B	A) False. $17 + 20 + 9 + 8 + 12 + 4 = 70$ students

B) True. $\dfrac{[17(11) + 20(12) + 9(13) + 8(14) + 12(15) + 4(16)]}{70} = \dfrac{900}{70} = 12.86$

C) False. The current median age is the average of the 35th and 36th numbers which is $\dfrac{12 + 12}{2} = 12$. If three sixteen year olds arrived the median number would be the 37th number which is 12. Therefore the median age would not change.

D) False. There are 33 students older than the mean of 12.86. Half of 70 would be 35 and 33 is less than 35. Therefore less than half of the students are older than the median.

Question No.	Answer	Detailed Explanation
5	B	A) False. The best fuel mileage recorded was 38 mpg.

B) True. The Interquartile range is from 27 – 34 mpg which contains 50% of the data.

C) False. The median fuel mileage was 31 mpg.

D) False. There are twelve data points in all which means that each quartile contains four points and the IQR contains two quartiles or eight points.

Question No.	Answer	Detailed Explanation
6	D	Note: Each tick mark is 2 inches.

A) False. About 25% of the trees were 7 feet 6 inches or taller.

B) False. Each quartile has the same number of data points.

C) False. The median height is 6 feet 4 inches.

D) True. If Q3 has 15 data points then so do Q1, Q2 and Q4. This makes a total of $15 * 4 = 60$ trees. We say "about" because the median may not be in a quartile.

Question No.	Answer	Detailed Explanation
7	C	A) False. There are 27 leaves which represent data for 27 students.
		B) False. The median number is the 14th number. This is 54.
		C) True. The greatest number of jumping jacks performed was 72 and the least was 30. $72 - 30 = 42$.
		D) False. There are six leaves in the 3 (30) stem which represents 6 students who performed less than 40 jumping jacks.

8	D	A) False The current mean of Tamryn's data is $\frac{[2(4) + 4(6) + 2(10) + 2(12)]}{10}$

$= \frac{76}{10} = 7.6$. If a 10 were added the new mean would be $\frac{[2(4) + 4(6) + 2(10) + 2(12) + 10]}{11} = \frac{86}{11} = 7.6$.

B) False. Tamryn: $\frac{[2(4) + 4(6) + 2(10) + 2(12)]}{10} = \frac{76}{10} = 7.8$.

Clio: $\frac{[2(6) + 2(7) + 3(8) + 9 + 2(10)]}{10} = \frac{79}{10} = 7.9$. Clio used more beads than Tamryn on the average.

C) False. As shown by the spread of the data, Tamryn's data has more variability than Clio's.

D) True. The median of Clio's data is 8. If Clio added another 8 the median would remain the same.

9	A	A) True. There are a total of $2 + 5 + 18 + 4 + 1 = 30$ days. 18 of these days had a temperature of $70 - 74°F$. This is more than half of the days.

B) False. $4 + 1 = 5$ days had temperatures above $74°F$. This is $\frac{5}{30} = 16.6\%$ which is less than 20%.

C) False. There is no way to determine the average temperature without specific data points.

D) False. There were $5 + 2 = 7$ days below $74°F$ and $4 + 1 = 5$ days above $74°F$. Therefore there were more days below $74°F$ than days above $74°F$.

10	B	A) False. The mean is

$\frac{4 + 6 + 9 + 10 + 13 + 14 + 17 + 17 + 17 + 18 + 20 + 20 + 22 + 22 + 25+31+34}{17} = \frac{299}{17}$

$= 17.59$. The median is 17. Therefore the mean is greater than the median.

B) True. The middle number is 17.
C) False. The range of fireflies is $34 - 4 = 30$.
D) False. Marcel caught fireflies on 17 nights.

Question No.	Answer	Detailed Explanation
11	Box 3	Because box 3 shows that 6 students in this class have 3 siblings. A smaller number of students have 0, 1, 2, 4, 5, or 6 siblings in this class.

12		

	10	14	17
Team 1: 15, 16, t, 17, 12, Mode = 17, What is t?			◉
Team 2: 7, 14, r, 16, 13 Mean = 12, What is r?	◉		
Team 3: 11, 7, 19, 14, z, Median = 14, What is z?		◉	

Team 1: $t = 17$ would be the mode because it would be listed two times.

Team 2: $(7 + 14 + r + 16 + 13) / 5 = 12$

$(50 + r) = 12 \times 5 = 60$

$r = 60 - 50 = 10$

Team 3: Arrange the known numbers in ascending order : 7, 11, 14, 19. It is given median is 14. Therefore, the unknown number z must be more than or equal to 14.

$z = 14$

GMAS FAQs

What will GMAS Assessment Look Like?

In many ways, the GMAS assessments will be unlike anything many students have ever seen. The tests will be conducted online, requiring students complete tasks to assess a deeper understanding of the Georgia standards. The students will take the Summative Assessment at the end of the year.

The time for the Math Summative assessment for each grade is given below:

Estimated Time on Task in Minutes		
Grade	Section 1	Section 2
3	65	65
4	65	65
5	65	65
6	65	65
7	65	65
8	65	65

How is this Lumos tedBook aligned to GMAS Guidelines?

The practice tests provided in the Lumos Program were created to reflect the depth and rigor of the GMAS assessments based on the information published by the test administrator. However, the content and format of the GMAS assessment that is officially administered to the students could be different compared to these practice tests. You can get more information about this test by visiting https://www.gadoe.org/Curriculum-Instruction-and-Assessment/Assessment/Pages/EOG-Study-Resource-Guides.aspx

What item types are included in the Online GMAS Test?

Because the assessment is online, the test will consist of a combination of new types of questions:

1. Selected Response or Multiple choice questions
2. Multi select or two part questions
3. Drag and Drop
4. Hot text
5. Equation editor
6. Plot the point
7. Bar chart

For more information on 2022-23 Assessment year, visit
http://www.lumoslearning.com/a/gmas-2022-faqs
OR Scan the **QR Code**

Discover Engaging and Relevant Learning Resources

Lumos EdSearch is a safe search engine specifically designed for teachers and students. Using EdSearch, you can easily find thousands of standards-aligned learning resources such as questions, videos, lessons, worksheets and apps. Teachers can use EdSearch to create custom resource kits to perfectly match their lesson objective and assign them to one or more students in their classroom.

To access the EdSearch tool, use the search box after you log into Lumos StepUp or use the link provided below.

www.lumoslearning.com/a/edsearchb

The Lumos Standards Coherence map provides information about previous level, next level and related standards. It helps educators and students visually explore learning standards. It's an effective tool to help students progress through the learning objectives. Teachers can use this tool to develop their own pacing charts and lesson plans. Educators can also use the coherence map to get deep insights into why a student is struggling in a specific learning objective.

Teachers can access the Coherence maps after logging into the StepUp Teacher Portal or use the link provided below.

www.lumoslearning.com/a/coherence-map

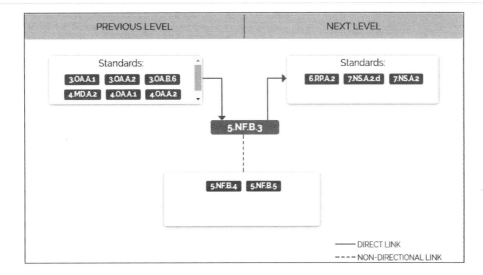

Progress Chart

Standard		Lesson	Page No.	Practice		Mastered	Re-practice /Reteach
GMAS	CCSS			Date	Score		
MGSE6.RP.1	6.RP.A.1	Expressing Ratios	9				
MGSE6.RP.2	6.RP.A.2	Unit Rates	14				
MGSE6.RP.3	6.RP.A.3	Solving Real World Ratio Problems	18				
MGSE6.RP.3b	6.RP.A.3.B	Solving Unit Rate Problems	22				
MGSE6.RP.3c	6.RP.A.3.C	Finding Percent	26				
MGSE6.RP.3d	6.RP.A.3.D	Measurement Conversion	30				
MGSE6.NS.1	6.NS.A.1	Division of Fractions	47				
MGSE6.NS.2	6.NS.B.2	Division of Whole Numbers	52				
MGSE6.NS.3	6.NS.B.3	Operations with Decimals	56				
MGSE6.NS.4	6.NS.B.4	Using Common Factors	60				
MGSE6.NS.5	6.NS.C.5	Positive and Negative Numbers	64				
MGSE6.NS.6a	6.NS.C.6.A	Representing Negative Numbers	68				
MGSE6.NS.6b	6.NS.C.6.B	Ordered Pairs	72				
MGSE6.NS.6c	6.NS.C.6.C	Number Line & Coordinate Plane	78				
MGSE6.NS.7	6.NS.C.7	Absolute Value	84				
MGSE6.NS.7b	6.NS.C.7.B	Rational Numbers in Context	87				
MGSE6.NS.7c	6.NS.C.7.C	Interpreting Absolute Value	92				
MGSE6.NS.7d	6.NS.C.7.D	Comparisons of Absolute Value	96				
MGSE6.NS.8	6.NS.C.8	Coordinate Plane	100				
MGSE6.EE.1	6.EE.A.1	Whole Number Exponents	129				
MGSE6.EE.2a	6.EE.A.2.A	Expressions Involving Variables	132				

Standard		Lesson	Page No.	Practice		Mastered	Re-practice /Reteach
GMAS	CCSS			Date	Score		
MGSE6.EE.2b	6.EE.A.2.B	Identifying Expression Parts	135				
MGSE6.EE.2c	6.EE.A.2.C	Evaluating Expressions	138				
MGSE6.EE.3	6.EE.A.3	Writing Equivalent Expressions	142				
MGSE6.EE.4	6.EE.A.4	Identifying Equivalent Expressions	145				
MGSE6.EE.5	6.EE.B.5	Equations and Inequalities	149				
MGSE6.EE.6	6.EE.B.6	Modeling with Expressions	153				
MGSE6.EE.7	6.EE.B.7	Solving One-Step Equations	157				
MGSE6.EE.8	6.EE.B.8	Representing Inequalities	161				
MGSE6.EE.9	6.EE.C.9	Quantitative Relationships	165				
MGSE6.G.1	6.G.A.1	Area	187				
MGSE6.G.2	6.G.A.2	Surface Area and Volume	193				
MGSE6.G.3	6.G.A.3	Coordinate Geometry	197				
MGSE6.G.4	6.G.A.4	Nets	204				
MGSE6.SP.1	6.SP.A.1	Statistical Questions	220				
MGSE6.SP.2	6.SP.A.2	Distribution	225				
MGSE6.SP.3	6.SP.A.3	Central Tendency	230				
MGSE6.SP.4	6.SP.B.4	Graphs & Charts	234				
MGSE6.SP.5	6.SP.B.5	Data Interpretation	242				
N/A	6.SP.B.5.B	Describing the Nature	247				
N/A	6.SP.B.5.C	Context of Data Gathered	251				
N/A	6.SP.B.5.D	Relating Data Distributions	255				

Grade **6**

✶ Lumos Learning
Developed by Expert Teachers

GEORGIA
ENGLISH
LANGUAGE ARTS LITERACY
GMAS Practice

Updated for 2022-23

(((tedBook)))
ONLINE

2 GMAS Practice Tests

7 Question Types

COVERS 40+ SKILLS

Available

- At Leading book stores
- Online www.LumosLearning.com

Made in the USA
Monee, IL
17 February 2023

28076089R00160